THE IAN BARCLAY STORY

GOING TO THE NTH DEGREE

Model of a private tennis coach
and his protégés
through thick and thin

MIKE SPRUZEN

THE IAN BARCLAY STORY
GOING TO THE NTH DEGREE

Copyright © MIKE SPRUZEN 2020

First published by Zeus Publications 2019
http://www.zeus-publications.com
P.O. Box 2554
Burleigh M.D.C.
QLD, 4220
Australia.

 A catalogue record for this book is available from the National Library of Australia

All Rights Reserved

No part of this book may be reproduced in any form, by photocopying or by any electronic or mechanical means, including information storage or retrieval systems, without permission in writing from both the copyright owner and the publisher of this book.

This book is a work of non-fiction.

The author asserts his moral rights.

ISBN: 978-1-920699-60-4

THE IAN BARCLAY STORY

GOING TO THE NTH DEGREE

A true legend and champion to the grassroots of Australian tennis

MIKE SPRUZEN

The Author

Mike Spruzen is a Tennis Australia Club Professional Coach and former pupil of Ian Barclay.

Mike has developed an enviable reputation in grassroots coaching, club and program development and mentoring of young players at introductory levels principally at Heatherdale Tennis Club and Bairnsdale Tennis Club and is currently coaching at Boroondara Tennis Centre.

Contents

Acknowledgements 5
Foreword 6
Author's Preface 7
Dedication 8
Introduction 9
Early Days and Formative Influences 10
Tennis 16
Romance 23
Coaching 26
In Demand 33
Ever-supportive Father 42
Broader Horizons 44
Back at Heatherdale 56
Patrick (Pat) Cash 59
Backyard Tennis Court 62
Davis Cup 66
The Playing Coach 73
Back Home 77
Returning Overseas 79
Full-time Touring Coach 81
The Championships, Wimbledon 86
Post Wimbledon 93
Barclay's Ultimate Competitor 97
Time off the Tour 101
The Split 107
An Offshore Opportunity 110
On The Road Again 114
Success in the Motherland 119
UK Success Down Under and Beyond 125
Eye for Talent 129
Down Time 131

Dark Clouds	134
Back to Oz	138
Other Talents	140
Official Appointments	145
Recognition	147
An About-Turn	149
Super 10s Junior Tennis	153
The Biggest Loss	155
Flying Solo Again	158
Continuing the Dream	162
Influences in UK	165
Following in Their Mentor's Footsteps	168
Interests, Friends and Family	170
Philosophy	175
Passion, Patience and Dedication	176
Postscript	179
Epilogue	180
Index	181

Acknowledgements

There have been many people, both within Australia and also overseas, who have assisted in the compilation of *The Ian Barclay Story, Going to the Nth Degree*. From family members to ex-students, playing partners, fellow coaches, and beyond, you have all helped enormously to make this story happen.

In particular, I would like to thank John Glynn, who came onto the scene to help me somewhat by chance. John and his family have been firmly entrenched in tennis for many years and whose value and contribution to the game I hold dearly. He saw a need for this story to be told and drove me to complete it.

To Dr Ann Quinn, for not only her part in this story, but whose advice and help in constructing Ian's story has been crucial and very much appreciated.

To Ian, who drank endless coffees with me as we dissected his history over many years.

In alphabetical order they are: Bradley Barclay, Dean Barclay, Ian Barclay, Jackie Barclay*, Janet Barclay, Toni-Ann Barclay, Graham Bland,* Alan Bray, Barry Brennan, Warren Brennan, Nick Brown, Jessie Burbridge, Bob Butterfield, Patrick Cash, Andrew Castle, Lee Childs, Will Coghlan, Belinda Colinari, Andrew Crossman, John Fitzgerald, Philip Fowler, John Glynn, Rohan Goetzke, Mark Hartnett, Will Heffernan, Wes Horskins, Kim Kachel, Katrina Kearney, Charles Kneale, Martin Kozma, Martin Lee, Rocky Loccisano, Jan MacDonald, Noel McMahon, Anne Minter, Jack Noseda, Kim O'Connor, Elizabeth Peers, Ann Quinn, Bernadette Randall, Shyan Sivaratnam, Geoff Spruzen,* Virginia Stacey, Geoff Stone, James Trotman, James Turner, Russell Watts and Steve Wood.

* Deceased

Foreword

Ian Barclay is a special individual.

Tennis has been privileged to have him in its industry.

It takes a rare coach to take a player from a young junior all the way to being a Grand Slam champion, almost unheard of in fact. Ian did this with Pat Cash.

He succeeded in this feat, but he did and continues to do so much more. His dedication to the improvement of all his students and prodigies has been a lifelong devotion. As one of Cashy's doubles partners along the way, I witnessed this first hand and was never not impressed with Ian's ethic and dedication.

'Barkers' is faithful beyond the meaning of the word. He cares not just about his students' tennis improvement but in their life journey as well. He believes that tennis players should also be quality people!

Ian is a living example of the traditions, values and work ethic that tennis wants to perpetuate in this sport that we love.

His contribution to Australian tennis is forever etched in its history.

John Fitzgerald OAM
Australian tennis legend
Former Australian Davis Cup captain and player

Author's Preface

From his childhood days as a keen junior footballer and mad Hawthorn supporter, through to his early working days as a working commercial artist and then on to his profession as a tennis coach, Ian Lawrence Barclay has been unique.

His time and dedication to developing young tennis players has seen few in the industry reach such parallels. From his grassroots beginnings, he has taken his students to the pinnacle of world tennis, in particular Patrick Cash, who captured the Wimbledon Men's Singles title in 1987.

Wholeheartedly supported throughout his journey by wife Jackie, Ian has connected with people from all walks of life and across the globe. His influences on so many in the tennis world have made such a difference.

In my mind, whatever he has put his efforts towards he has always gone to the nth degree.

It has been my honour and privilege to tell Ian Barclay's story.

Dedication

In loving memory of Jackie.

For whom, without her love and dedication,

none of this story could possibly have been told.

Ian

Introduction

"Get your first serve in! You must make your return! Whatever you do, don't hit the net! Never ever, ever lob on match point! Come on, move your feet!"

These pertinent tennis coaching clichés have emanated from the mouth of Australian professional tennis coach Ian Lawrence Barclay at local, national and international tennis levels, week in week out for nearly 50 years.

They have been imparted timely and wisely to hundreds of young tennis players across the globe, whose endeavours have ranged from dreaming of becoming world champions, to being the best players they can be, to just loving the sport, or simply just wanting to improve their level of tennis.

Early Days and Formative Influences

Ian Barclay, known affectionately as Mr B or Barkers to all who have known him, was born on December 2nd 1938, the second of two children, to parents Roy and Ethel Barclay. Ian's elder sister, Janet, was born three years earlier. The children were raised in Beech Street, East Malvern, an inner eastern suburb of Melbourne.

Growing up during the Second World War and the subsequent economic turbulence which followed, the children's grandparents, Arthur and Jessica Barclay were surprisingly well off.

Starting out, a young Ian

They owned two jewellery stores, one in the north-east Victorian country town of Wangaratta and the other on iconic Bourke Street, in the heart of Melbourne's business district. They also owned a tannery, where Ian and Janet's Aunty Ivy ran the finances and their Aunty Vera designed furs, some being for a number of leading local film actors.

To understand much about Ian, one need only look at the two generations of the Barclay family that preceded him. Arthur Barclay was a generous man who treated his employees well. He occasionally gave them a bit extra in their pay packets, as recognition for their hard work. He often took them down to the local hotel after work where he would shout each a beer, Arthur himself also being quite partial to a drink. He used the four edges of a nearby billiard table on which to distribute a mass of coins, from which the thirsty workers could then help themselves. An interesting and adventurous man, he was a collector of indigenous artefacts. He also dabbled in gold prospecting, often spending time digging in the Gippsland regional town of Walhalla. At one time Roy Barclay was so convinced that Arthur had hidden a sizeable amount of gold somewhere in Walhalla, that he took his son on several trips there, armed with a spade and shovel to try and locate the treasure. Ian long joked that their failure to ever find any evidence of the alleged booty may well explain why he still works to this very day.

Roy Barclay was a metallurgist by trade, but worked as an aviation mechanic. During the Second World War, one of his major tasks was, as an inspector, to conduct maintenance on government aircraft. On being employed in that division, he was not required to go off to war like many of his mates, but due to the demands of the job he was frequently away from home. That didn't preclude the rest of the Barclays from having to do the all too familiar trench drills close to the family home while the war raged on elsewhere.

Like his own father, Roy too was adventurous. One of his favourite pastimes was to go camping in the bush to snare rabbits. Also a keen fisherman, it was not uncommon for him to load young Ian, Janet and their friends into the family car, an old 1928 Graham-Paige Model 610 sedan, and head off to the beach. A clever man, to save on expenses during hard times he would start the car on petrol, then change over and run it on cheaper kerosene. With the traditional dickey seat in the rear, the large straight six-engine motor car had room for nine people. Such was its size, one year Roy squeezed young Ian's entire junior football team on board. Years later, when he got his own driver's licence, Ian often piled his friends into his father's car and headed off to the local dance. Roy was also a trainer for runners competing in the prestigious Victorian country athletics event, the Easter Stawell Gift, as well as for umpires in the Victorian Football League (VFL).

Ian's father was a hard worker and perfectionist in his field. Highly principled, he would not stand for any nonsense and had a strong sense of respect for friends and those within the community. Good manners in and outside the family household were mandatory. The simple adage of giving up a seat on the train for an elderly citizen was an act of decency and the done thing. The family dressed well for all occasions.

Ian's mother, Ethel was born in Manchester, England. She worked as a dressmaker. A quiet woman by nature, she was slight of build yet very nimble, especially around the house. As a typical youngster, Ian occasionally let fly with a bit of backchat. Also having no tolerance for misbehaviour, she would quickly grab the nearby straw broom and take off after her son, ready to give out some punishment. The family lived a healthy lifestyle and homemade meals were the norm, as there was no such thing as takeaway food at the time. Ethel had the knack of kicking an Australian Rules football with a fair degree of skill. Mother and son often played kick to kick in the backyard before dinner.

Ian and Janet both attended the local Lloyd Street Primary School. They got on well as siblings, but a competitive Ian often teased his elder sister, sometimes mercilessly. In her words, he was "the typical rotten little brother. Usually he was bright and easy-going but could not stand to lose at anything." She would occasionally let him win a sporting battle, just to avoid hearing the associated tantrum that would follow a defeat.

Football and cricket were the most popular sports chosen by boys of the time. Living only two streets apart, primary school friend and football club team mate Noel McMahon and Ian regularly engaged in neighbourhood contests. When challenges arose, both boys formed teams and McMahon and his mates often held the upper hand against the determined younger Barclay.

With not much money to go around during their childhood days, the family car was selectively used. Therefore, the Barclay children often had to ride their pushbikes if they wanted to go anywhere. To earn money, Ian used his bike to do a paper round for the local newsagent and deliver groceries for the greengrocer. He also used local trams to help deliver prescriptions to pensioners on behalf of the local chemist. In doing so, he jumped on and off the trams' running boards as they moved up and down the street.

For their secondary education, Janet attended the Methodist Ladies College (MLC) in Kew, while Ian went to Caulfield Technical School. Of the two, Janet was the academic and enjoyed artistic pursuits, while Ian's interests were in sport and art. Sport though, in particular, football was his passion. It didn't necessarily matter in which field it was, day in and day out, he could not get enough. Both children also loved dancing and they became quite accomplished. The jive was Ian's speciality. He would readily grab Janet if she was nearby in the family home and swing her around his body and between his legs in true dance fashion. Janet loved to ice skate at the local St Moritz ice skating rink and the money she earned from doing housework regularly covered her two shillings entry fee into the arena.

Roy suffered somewhat from his association with the war, while the children's mother at one point contracted a bout of tuberculosis, a common ailment of the times. It required her having six months' convalescence in a sanatorium alongside others with the same complaint. To help ease the burden on the family, Ian was sent to live with his father's brother, Uncle Leo, and his family for six months, in the northern Victorian country town of Tocumwal. He went to the local school and played football, captaining the town's junior team.

Leo Barclay worked for the State Government's Department of Main Roads. To help his uncle out, Ian often drove the work truck, albeit illegally as he was too young to own a licence. He helped with the family chores, regularly cutting up nearby red gum wood for his Aunty Iris' kitchen stove and the family room fire. Janet remained in Melbourne to look after the cooking and domestic duties for the children's father.

Like most boys, Ian wanted to play league football in the VFL, with the ultimate dream of playing with his beloved club, Hawthorn. Back in Melbourne, he played his junior football for the local East Malvern Football Club. The legendary Tom Hafey, four-time premiership coach of VFL side Richmond during the 1960s and '70s, played in the club's senior side. Ian played alongside Hafey's younger brother, Peter, in the Under 15s. Although lightly built, he was particularly fast across the ground and loved nothing more than to take a spectacular overhead mark atop a pack of players. Such was his love of the game, Ian regularly waited around after finishing his morning match, hoping that one of the senior players wouldn't take the field for the afternoon game so that he might get a chance to play again. However, due to his light frame he also had a tendency to get knocked around physically.

One unfortunate week, he incurred a serious injury where he damaged the coccyx bone in his lower back. Disappointingly, it was enough to curtail his competitive football playing days and therefore any real prospects of a future career at the highest level.

Away from the football field, Ian found another sporting interest in horse racing. It stemmed from his uncle Leo Roddy's involvement as a Starting Price (SP) Bookmaker. A family friend offered the young teenager the job of finding out the starting prices for each race at the Caulfield Racecourse and to then ring them through to the SP Bookmaker from outside the track. A mid-week race meeting meant he had to wag school in order to fulfil the offer. He was also warned that there was a chance he may get caught, as it was an illegal practice. He got paid around £5 for his efforts, which ironically, was more than he got paid for his first real job. He did it for a time and earned a handy sum of money.

One day, however, things didn't quite go according to plan. Just after the fourth race when he was due to ring through the next set of starting prices, Ian was making his way on to the course via his usual route past an old oak tree tucked away in a quiet corner, in order to get the prices. He noticed some police standing adjacent to the railway line close by. As he got over the fence, he was converged upon by a number of detectives wearing traditional pork pie hats and informed he was a person of interest. Initially unaware what was happening, instinct kicked in and Ian decided to take off down a main entrance, only to be stopped by police coming the other way. On being caught, he was taken down to the local police station and was strongly urged to hand over the bookie's telephone number. He had, however, been sworn to secrecy. Unable to get a confession, one policeman produced a rolled-up wet towel, then began to repeatedly hit him across the head and body. Ian finally decided he would give over someone else's telephone number, if only to get some relief from the continued flogging. The number was a fake. The local sergeant on duty, who had a fair bit to do with Ian's football club and was known by his father, meekly stood aside while the young boy took the beating.

On his son's return home, Roy was furious. Not just with Ian, but also with the police for the punishment they had given out and the marks left on the boy's face. It was decided the incident would remain a secret from Ian's mother. However, Barclay Senior didn't let the incident rest there. He put his teenage son into the back of the Graham-Paige and drove straight to the police station, whereupon he marched through the front door. A quiet man by nature, Roy flew into a rage, bashing his fist on the front desk, demanding why a boy so young should be subject to such treatment. Such was his anger he threatened to use his shotgun on the perpetrators.

A week later, a man wearing a dark suit, sunglasses and sporting a distorted nose arrived at Ian's school, approached him and handed over an envelope. Inside was a wad of cash and a telephone number. The amount of cash made him feel like a millionaire. He was informed that he could never run the starting prices again for fear of exposing the bookie, but by not giving out on his former employer he had protection on his doorstep should he ever require it. Young Ian hadn't realised that what he had got involved in was a criminal offence. However, it didn't stop him from maintaining an interest in racing and he continued to go to meetings with his tennis mates, though avoiding Caulfield for a time.

Having finished her secondary schooling, Janet Barclay completed a Business Diploma, then went on to work in the fashion industry. She harboured a greater desire to become an airline hostess and ultimately got a job with Trans Australian Airlines, where she worked for two years before getting married.

Barclay completed his Diploma of Art at Swinburne Technical College in Hawthorn, which he had taken up after finishing secondary school. He decided he wanted to become a commercial artist.

The printing firm that his best mate Keith Thorpe worked for – Wrightsell – offered Barclay an apprenticeship. He worked hard designing artwork and pushing his paintbrush. A work colleague who had been in the industry for many years took notice of the new employee and offered up a suggestion. Seeing the young apprentice had plenty of ideas, but was a little rough around the edges, the co-worker suggested to Barclay that he might take up a Dale Carnegie course with the view to helping him learn how better to communicate with people in the course of his work, deliver a good sales pitch and develop a strong memory for names. Barclay took up the suggestion. One of his major tasks during the course was to get up in front of a crowd and talk cold for 15 minutes on an impromptu topic.

Barclay continued to work as a commercial artist for the next 17 years. For nine of those he worked for a company called Colourprint, an arm of the well-known MacRobertsons Chocolate Manufacturing Company. A takeover of the company and subsequent loss of jobs for many of his workmates led Barclay to also move on. He then worked for Noel McMahon's kitchenware importing business as a freelance artist in the marketing presentation department.

Tennis

Aged 15, Ian took to playing tennis. Like most boys of the time, he'd previously had scant regard for the sport, thinking of it as a bit of a sissy's game. Ironically, having little desire to play, he bought his first tennis racquet, a Spalding Top Flite, from the earnings raised from his part-time jobs.

About 20 children from the neighbourhood organised a singles tournament at the local Airdrie Park Tennis Club. Neighbour Noel McMahon thought he was going well when he defeated a young boy called Bernie Massey, who would later play VFL football with Melbourne, 6-0. He then came up against an athletic Ian, who surprisingly gained a bit of competitive revenge and promptly despatched McMahon by the same margin. The young newcomer to the game went into the final a raging favourite, only to be brought down by a very good junior named Lindsay Perott.

Ian joined another local club in East Malvern called the Lockie Tennis Club, where he played some night tennis. He took up coaching lessons with well-known Professional Tennis Association Victoria (PTAV) coach Brian Slattery at the South Yarra tennis courts. Slattery was also coaching two talented brothers, Neale and John Fraser, both of whom would go on to have varying degrees of success on the world stage.

From there, Ian's love for the game grew and he soon realised tennis was the sport he wanted to concentrate most on. He only had the basic equipment; however, he did have plenty of willing practice partners to choose from around the neighbourhood.

Keith Thorpe decided to take him along to the inner suburban St. Kilda Tennis Club to play. While there, they often practised for hours.

Ian's serve, however, caused him some concerns. After each hit with Thorpe he would go home, set down a jam tin on the ground in front of his feet and use it as a target for the purpose of practising the ball toss on his serve. He wanted to perfect it.

Keith Thorpe with Ian

From his early practice sessions with Keith Thorpe, St Kilda Tennis Club became Barclay's first Lawn Tennis Association of Victoria (LTAV) pennant club.

He started in 'D' Grade, but initially found the competition to be a struggle, much tougher to adapt to than he had expected. He knew he was quick, so retrieving shots wasn't an issue. He wanted to both understand and learn how to play the game better.

The good players around Barclay urged him to play steadily, keep the ball in play and wait for the shorter mid-court ball to approach the net to execute his volleys.

The continental grip of the day helped his preferred serve and volley game, which by and large was the norm amongst players. It gave him a nice feel for his shots.

From each match he played, he improved and thus became more educated. In his second season, Barclay moved up to 'C Special' Grade. He learned to play to his strengths and felt that tactically if he could play the ball in behind his opponent, especially to the backhand side that got them off balance, it would offer up the chance to approach the net. He would avoid getting readily passed and could finish the point off with his volley or smash. As he developed, the backhand volley, smash and drop shot became his favourite shots.

From St Kilda, Barclay and Thorpe then moved to the more established East Malvern Tennis Club where Barclay played pennant for the next 20 years. The move to East Malvern saw him link up once again with neighbour Noel McMahon and strike up friendships with other players such as Barry Brennan, Mike King and Ray O'Connor. It became common knowledge around the tennis circles that Barclay had two strong assets – his fitness and speed. McMahon felt this was in part due to his light frame as well as the tough training drills he had endured while playing football. The more he played the game, Barclay noticed some of his contemporaries holding their forehand drive grips more towards the eastern side of the continental grip. Thus he saw more topspin used during rallies.

At 17 years of age, Barclay was playing a much higher level of tennis. He decided to try his hand on the tournament scene and headed off with several of his East Malvern friends to Daylesford in north-west country Victoria for the Annual Labour Day holiday tournament, played on lawn. The fun-loving Barry Brennan was a few years older than Barclay and owned a car. When he picked Ian up from his parents' home, Roy stood at the front door. He gave Brennan a cautionary warning to look after his son. Brennan looked back and cheekily replied, "Yes, Roy, no worries, she'll be right." It was common practice for the East Malvern lads to get their kicks not only on the tennis court, but off it as well. Brennan would have enough trouble taking care of himself, let alone keeping a close eye on his younger pennant team mate.

In his first tournament, Barclay excelled. He reached the Men's Open Singles Final and defeated Dendy Park 'A' Grade pennant player Howard Ellis to take the title. He also won the doubles and mixed doubles events.

Daylesford became an annual event. As money was tight, Barclay and his tennis mates regularly sought out the cheapest accommodation available. The local Belvedere Hotel suited their needs. Some of Barclay's friends included O'Connor, Billy Mahon and Gerald Shoet. Mahon owned a 1948 Ford Prefect car, which he took along to the tournaments. Barclay and Mahon often went out before a day's matches to shoot rabbits. One year, they returned from a morning out carrying a dead black snake. Barclay draped the snake over a spare coat hanger and hung it inside the door of Mahon's car, knowing full well Egyptian-born Shoet had a hatred of snakes. They waited for Shoet to get into the car in preparation to head off for the day's tennis. Suddenly the boys heard an anguished cry and threats in both English and Egyptian to kill whoever was responsible for the prank. Moments later, they turned to see the startled Shoet tearing down the street on foot in the opposite direction.

Not one to easily forget, Shoet organised the group to steal Barclay's towel and clothes one night while he was showering after his final match of the day and then lock him out of his hotel room. In those days it was common to have only one shared communal shower on any one floor of a hotel. They hid his clothes, leaving Barclay abandoned in the corridor, soaked and without a stitch on. The only thing he could find to help cover up was a large leaf from a nearby pot plant. The boys sat in hiding, laughing uncontrollably, waiting for him to be caught in his near-naked state.

Barclay's competitive spirit kicked in. He talked the young hotel employee who had found him wearing just a plant leaf into giving him a spare key to Shoet's room. Waiting for his chance, he smuggled an outdoor garden hose inside his sports bag and into his hotel room. Late the same night he quietly crept into Shoet's room, passed by his sleeping mate and into the bathroom, where he connected the hose to a tap. The cold Daylesford night air meant the water temperature was freezing. Barclay then poked the end of the hose under the bedsheets between Shoet's sizeable bare feet, went back to the bathroom and turned the tap on fully. Once again, the familiar shrieks of anguish could be heard, but this time all around the hotel. Barclay quickly dived out of the room. Although found out, revenge had been sweet. Dramatically one year later, the Belvedere Hotel mysteriously caught fire and was severely damaged. At one stage, the finger was wrongly and unjustifiably pointed at Barclay's group simply because celebrations during one of his title wins were deemed to have gotten more than just a little out of hand.

While Barclay was playing a doubles match with Keith Thorpe, a young calf strayed onto the court from the neighbouring paddock. Thorpe grabbed the animal by the neck and tail and ran it off the court. Barclay rolled around the court in laughter. Thorpe returned and on playing his next shot, his racquet slipped and flew from his hand. He had forgotten to clean off the present the uninvited guest had left him with.

Barclay and his friends travelled to other country tournaments such as Echuca, Warrnambool and Warragul. There was a tournament held every long weekend and they did the rounds of them all. Friendships evolved farther and wider. If they could afford the time and money, the young tennis players sometimes ventured on to places like Mildura for a further couple of days just to unwind, away from the tennis courts.

Ray O'Connor had a Volkswagen car and it provided both he and Ian with plenty of fun and at times hair-raising adventures. On one trip to the Benalla country tournament, they were driving up through the beautiful Pretty Sally region in Victoria's Strathbogie Ranges when Barclay seeing smoke billowing from the rear, remarked to O'Connor he thought the car was on fire. Sure enough, the engine, which in Volkswagens were situated at the rear, had caught alight. Quickly deciding their next move, they hailed down a motorbike rider and offered up some cash if he would take their empty petrol can to the next town and return it full of oil. The young tennis players thought they themselves had been taken for a ride when there was no sign of the returning biker over the next couple of hours. The Good Samaritan finally returned and between the three they managed to restart the car.

Barclay was a member of the 1958 East Malvern 'B' Grade winning pennant team, which included close friend Brennan. A subsequent season with Noel McMahon in the same grade realised another premiership.

Four days prior to his 21st birthday, while again travelling in Ray O'Connor's car, Barclay suffered a near-fatal accident.

The pair had been to a dance on St Kilda Road one Saturday night and had not long dropped off two girls they had met there to their bayside Sandringham homes.

Ian and Jackie with family friends, Ray and Judy O'Connor

They were returning home, when suddenly they were met head on by a 1950's Studebaker, which had made a right-hand turn directly into their path. O'Connor managed to escape with relatively minor injuries. However, Barclay wasn't so fortunate.

He was thrown through the front windscreen, before somehow recoiling back inside. Fortunately, O'Connor's toolbox, which had been lying on the back seat, narrowly missed both young men when it flew between them, also smashing through the front window. Barclay was thrown back outside again, this time through the passenger door. He was badly injured, his legs and chest severely lacerated, face smashed with several teeth lost. A piece of glass was pressed up against a main artery in his neck and with the injuries already sustained, couldn't stop the rapid blood flow. Lying in the gutter on what was a wet and rainy night, he later attributed a passing young sea scout to saving his life. The calm youngster was able to compress the wound until the ambulance arrived.

Facing microsurgery and with a face covered in stitches, a determined Barclay told his father he was going to make it to his own birthday, whatever the circumstance. He did, albeit heavily medicated. He held out till around 11 pm before passing out in front of his guests. Barclay required months of treatment, including endless rounds of plastic surgery. Once rehabilitated, his tennis mates threw light-hearted barbs at him, having found out that much of the skin for his grafts had been taken from his backside. In later years, he would be reminded of the accident in the most innocuous of ways. In his 22nd year, Barclay bought his first car, a Ford Zephyr Six. A promotion to 'B Special' pennant saw him win yet another flag.

One of Barclay's best friends and tennis contemporaries at the time was Will Coghlan. Their association began during their pennant days when Barclay played for East Malvern, and Coghlan for Glen Iris Valley Tennis Club. Coghlan was one of the best pennant players that Barclay saw. Relatively light in stature, he hit the ball cleanly and possessed a deadly accurate return of serve. Unlike many, Coghlan travelled abroad in 1960 and 1961 to further improve his game, courtesy of some private sponsorship. He had some impressive wins against seasoned world-class players in Grand Slam events.

Although managing good results, the financial return from playing amateur tennis in that era was meagre at best. A player of Coghlan's ilk may have earned only around five pounds sterling a day in Britain. "After six months away you did well if you broke even," said Coghlan. He was billeted out by host families and joked they would always ask him when was he going to get a real job, as there was no money in tennis. It was reason enough for him to eventually decide to get himself a job back home in Australia. In all, Coghlan contested 13 main draw Australian Opens and recorded some fine wins over the likes of top English players Roger Taylor and Mike Sangster and up-and-coming Aussies Ray Ruffels and Allan Stone. He took future great John Newcombe to the brink, twice losing in five sets. Back on the domestic scene he won the Victorian Hardcourt Singles title three times.

Unsure how his friend Barclay would have performed overseas, particularly on the European clay, Coghlan believed he would have more than held his own on the doubles court. "Ian was outstanding at the net, with a super volley and a very reliable smash. He could use his groundstrokes well enough to make his way to the net, which was where he excelled most." Barclay more than held his own against his local contemporaries and may well have gone abroad to test his talent against the world's best, but chose to stay at home due to a combination of the cost involved in overseas travel, his looming marriage, and the commencement of a family.

Barclay continued playing country tournaments and made regular trips up to the northern Victoria town of Echuca for the Annual Easter Tournament. Through the 1960s, '70s and '80s he collected a string of singles, doubles and mixed doubles titles.

In 1970, Barclay partnered Noel McMahon in the Men's Open Doubles event. Although a more than accomplished player in his own right, McMahon knew he was clearly the second best player on the court, dragged along by the competitive Barclay through the draw until they reached the final. There they met pennant contemporaries Barry Brennan and John Keller against whom, after a great tussle they eventually held a match point. McMahon, who played the backhand side, committed, in Barclay's view, one of tennis' most heinous crimes; he sent up a short lob. The smash was duly hit by Keller for a clean winner. Unimpressed, Barclay turned to McMahon and yelled, "MACCA, YOU BLOODY DILL – NEVER, EVER LOB ON MATCH POINT." McMahon looked around for the closest hole to crawl down. Fortunately, match point arose again and they won it to take the title.

For years after, the humorous McMahon joked that the locals at the Moama Hotel, situated a few kilometres away across the Murray River, could even hear Barclay's voice that day and reminded him of it when they returned there later after the day's matches. Like many who played the game of doubles alongside Barclay, a player could well feel the wrath if one committed any one of the game's cardinal sins, particularly at a crucial moment during a match. Here was a serious competitor and a potential coach in the making.

Romance

Barclay was still having bouts of post-accident facial surgery when he met the love of his life, a young girl at the Powerhouse weekly dance at Albert Park in South Melbourne, during the summer of 1960. Her name was Jacqueline Mary Naismith. Known as Jackie, she and her two younger siblings, Kay and Jimmy, had been raised in the inner Melbourne suburb of Richmond.

Kay, Ian and Jackie pictured at Powerhouse

She attended St Ignatius Primary School before moving onto the neighbouring secondary girls' school, Vaucluse Convent.

Like Ian, she loved sport. Her interests were in playing softball, basketball, netball and tennis. Softball was her first love and she played at both the Fawkner Park and Waverley fields, situated on either side of town. Jackie was also a youth leader at the local Richmond Youth Club, which helped teach young wayward adolescent children about the benefits of playing sport. She had the unique fortune to meet the great American Olympic athlete Jessie Owens through the club. Her brother Jimmy played reserves VFL football for the Richmond Football Club. Her younger sister was named Kay. Like Ian, Jackie also loved dancing, having started classes from the age of four.

In their early courting days, Jackie went along to watch Ian's pennant tennis matches at East Malvern and he, her softball and basketball games. Jackie's involvement in basketball sparked his interest, so much so that he gathered up some of his pennant tennis mates including Colin Stubbs and Geoff Osborne and they began playing competition basketball at Albert Park. This lasted five seasons. Raised as an Essendon supporter, Jackie soon found herself in the 'Hawks' nest alongside a Hawthorn-mad Ian.

On 10th September 1962, Ian and Jackie were married at the Wesley Methodist Church in Melbourne. Keith Thorpe was Ian's best man and Barry Brennan his groomsman.

It was common practice that the bridegroom and his party each wear a pair of white gloves. Brennan forgot his pair on arriving at the service. Come the time for wedding photographs, he was the odd one out. Thorpe and Brennan hatched a plan. They decided to share a glove each and made sure they stood at the each end of the bridal party line, with only the gloved hand showing. It worked and no one was any more the wiser.

Rear: Jackie, Ian, Dean, *Front:* Toni-Ann and Brad

In 1965, the first of the Barclay's three children, son Dean was born, followed by second son Bradley in 1968. The couple's third child, daughter Toni-Ann was born in 1969.

Jackie admired Ian's athletic ability, his talent as a tennis player and above all his absolute love of the game. In his mid-20s, she saw him play a match against top seed and multiple Grand Slam titleholder, Roy Emerson, in the second round of the 1965 Australian Open, played at the then home Australian tennis, Kooyong. Although Emerson was the better player and won comfortably, she felt Ian showed plenty through his sheer competitive spirit. Through his early competitive days, Ian used Dunlop rackets and, like others of the day, was often asked to play in exhibition matches as a means of promoting the company's brand.

Horse racing was a favourite pastime of Barclay's and a timely trip to the Moonee Valley Racecourse with tennis mate Bert Kearney proved fruitful. Kearney urged Barclay to place a double bet in the fifth race. Barclay was reluctant but before he knew it, Kearney had slipped him £1 and sent him on his way to lay the bet. Courtesy of a win, that £1 became £500.

Upon greeting Jackie back at home, he opened his jacket and out flew a great wad of notes. A number of other good wins at the track during that year went a long way towards the young couple buying their first home. With money tight, any racetrack earnings quickly found their way into the bank. He had a dream to one day of owning his own racehorse.

With East Malvern Tennis Club friend Charlie White's help in financing the remainder of the purchase, Ian and Jackie bought their first house in Sesame Street, Mt Waverley, situated in Melbourne's eastern suburbs. In the 1960s, apple orchards were quite prominent in the area and there was one at the end of the street. Roy Barclay often drove young grandson Brad up and down it on his knee in his car to check the apples on the trees.

Coaching

Roy Barclay was a friend of Ewen Denny, President of the Studfield Tennis Club (these days called Knox City Tennis Club), located in the eastern suburbs. He mentioned to Denny that Ian had shown some interest in helping young children learn to play the game. Studfield didn't have a coach at the time, so before long Ian started conducting lessons part-time at the club two nights a week, while still working his day job.

The idea of tennis coaching sat well with Barclay. He had watched some of the greats of the game and studied them closely. His favourite player was Lew Hoad, whose simple, uncomplicated technique allowed him to do anything with the ball. Barclay believed he had learned enough through playing the game, observing others in matches and being coached himself, that he could now help young players learn some of the nuances of the game. He felt he understood the shape of the swings, could see what worked well or didn't and had the ability to get to the source of a problem and correct it. Many of his students at Studfield had basic hand-eye coordination issues. He wanted to find ways to improve this basic fundamental and in the process make them better players.

Barclay decided he would leave the commercial art trade if and when an opportunity arose that allowed him to make tennis coaching a more full-time, professional career. This decision was timely as it coincided with another nearby eastern suburban tennis club, the Heatherdale Tennis Club, located in Mitcham, appraising its own coaching position. With the suburb's population growing, it believed the time was right for it to appoint a full-time coach in preference to its existing part-time arrangement. It so happened that Barclay's name was raised in conversation between the club's Chairman of selectors, Graham Bland, and top line local player, Trevor Davidson, at a barbecue one evening. On the strength of Davidson's recommendation Bland organised a meeting with Barclay, himself and other committee members at the local Manhattan Hotel in Ringwood. With the club having yet to officially advertise the position, the group was more than impressed by the slight-of-build, moustached, prematurely grey-haired, part-time coach and his future vision. In August of the winter of 1973, the Heatherdale Tennis Club appointed Ian Barclay as its new full-time professional tennis coach. Typical of the club's social strength, a committee dinner was held at the Bland house to welcome the new coach and his family. The small gathering quickly grew as more and more club members dropped by to welcome Barclay into the fold. The decision to appoint Barclay would now be put to the test. He was off and running.

Originally founded by legendary Australian Davis Cup captain, Harry Hopman, at a public meeting and launch in 1966, the Heatherdale Tennis Club was a moderate-sized club with six traditional Victorian en tout cas tennis courts (a scoria-based crushed-brick shifting surface, with medium bounce and speed) and had junior and senior teams represented in the Eastern Metropolitan Region Lawn Tennis Association's weekday and weekend competitions. It also had a large number of social players utilising the courts.

The new appointment coincided with the upcoming 'A' Grade pennant grand final, to be held four days later, involving Barclay. He had not long moved to the Melbourne Cricket Club (MCC) to play the highest level competition which his previous club of 20 years, East Malvern, could not offer. Playing alongside Will Coghlan, Dr John Fraser (who had gone on to reach the Wimbledon Singles semi-final in 1962) and Tony Ryan, they won the final. As part of his introduction to Heatherdale and a chance for its members to see their new coach in action, a demonstration match between the four winning 'A' Grade pennant team mates was held the day before Barclay commenced coaching duties. A healthy turnout witnessed a top level, highly competitive match.

Barclay commenced his new coaching role on Monday 10th September, 1973. Each day Jackie loaded children Dean, Brad and Toni-Ann into the family car and drove the 20-minute trip to Heatherdale from Mt Waverley, where she attended to all the administration duties from court side. Graham Bland helped out with the accounts and also took enquiries for coaching at his nearby newsagency. Before long, student numbers started to grow, as did the new coach's time spent at the club.

Early on, Barclay kept his hand in at East Malvern most notably by taking out three Men's Open Singles Club Championship titles between 1971 and 1975. To supplement his initial work at Heatherdale, he coached at his former pennant club on Wednesdays after school with a group of its advanced players. As coaching concluded at 7 pm each Monday at Heatherdale, Barclay also took on extra work during the evening, coaching students at Monash University.

Barclay worked alone and openly demonstrated the strong work ethic he had inherited from both his father and grandfather. He left no stone unturned in his endeavour to improve each student's level of tennis. Professional tennis coaches analyse and correct players' technique and movement on a day-to-day basis. If Barclay saw a strength in a shot, he would help build the player's game around it. If a stroke didn't look classically perfect, but worked, he would just enhance it. On wet coaching nights, he took his students indoors, talked to them about the rules of the game in an entertaining way that kept them enthralled. He brought in videos of the world's best players, from which they could watch and learn.

Serve

Forehand Drive

Backhand Drive

Forehand Volley

Smash

Backhand Volley

Captions of Ian Barclay demonstrating different shot techniques in 1973

Barclay believed the only real way to properly assess his players was to watch them play matches, particularly when under pressure. One could look great in practice but that could amount to nothing when placed in a competitive situation. He would then correct whatever was needed. At the time, various local junior tournaments used a round-robin format, which enabled him to watch his players play multiple matches. He felt the format suited those players capable of competing, as the more matches they played, the more they would learn about the game and he about them.

Barclay now firmly believed that the time spent coaching at his other clubs and this new grassroots coaching opportunity at Heatherdale would be the ideal grounding for his new career. It soon became clear to both Ian and Jackie that they needed to move the family closer to the tennis club.

They bought their second house in Longland Rd, Mitcham, where they remained for the next eight years. The children were enrolled at the nearby Antonio Park Primary School, with daughter Toni-Ann, the youngest, aged five. They enjoyed the new move, where they played freely outside the house after school with their new classmates and neighbourhood friends. They played in nearby bushland and rode their bikes home when it was time for dinner. Everyone looked out for everyone else's children in the street.

All three Barclay children went to Fawkner Park to follow their mother's softball matches and often to the carnivals that involved interstate and international teams. Toni-Ann took to playing the game under her mother's wing. Jackie had already put together a distinguished career, which included being selected in the Victorian State representative team, twice as a catcher.

Newly elected Heatherdale President, Alan Bray, soon noticed the influx of juniors coming to the club and into the new coaching program, as did the person charged with the organisation of junior competition tennis at the club, convenor Geoff Spruzen.

Word had begun to spread around the neighbourhood about the club's new coach and the impact he was having. Bray took careful note of Barclay's seemingly innate ability to relate to his pupils.

Bray said, "Barkers had a great rapport with each child he took on. He could just as easily talk about how they were going at school, their football team or family as discuss a change in technique and the reasons for it.

"He showed he could communicate with players at each and every level. He showed great empathy with any child suffering from any form of mental or physical disability. It was clear in the children's eyes that Mr B had become everything to them and they wanted to impress him. At the same time he would readily reign in a troublesome pupil if need be, with a quiet, yet strong-worded approach.

"At times it was just a glare and a pupil knew where they stood. No one spoke back to the coach. There was a collective respect. He had great peripheral vision, knowing how his students were performing on distant courts. The standard of junior tennis at the club began to lift from the ground floor up."

Together the coach and junior convenor implemented a new weekday after-school competition for those youngsters 10 and under years of age who could serve, rally and move around the court sufficiently well enough, but were just below the level required to play the Association's Saturday morning official junior competition.

Fun, involvement and learning the game were the key objectives. The new innovation also helped to ease the burden on numbers wanting to play tennis. Teams played using the names of Australian tennis greats such as Rod Laver, John Newcombe, Ken Rosewall and Tony Roche and played a format along similar lines to their weekend counterparts.

The midweek ladies, several of whom were mothers of the new competition's children, gave greatly of their time to assist.

Geoff Spruzen saw the quality of coaching reach a new level and subsequently a swell in demand for positions in the club's junior teams. The juniors went from having six teams to 16 teams almost overnight. He specifically sought Barclay's assessment of prospective new competition players.

Jackie Barclay stood watching a Saturday morning junior match when a young player's mother standing nearby commented to her that it was pretty easy to see the influence that her husband's coaching was already having on the kids. They could all volley.

Twelve months into his new job, Barclay had to deal with one rather unsavoury off-court situation. He was made aware by some of his students that the driver of an ice cream van had parked alongside the courts one recent weekend and had been showing some pictures to young local boys and girls.

Barclay became a bit suspicious. Arriving for coaching one afternoon, the van showed up around the same time, not long after school finishing time, and parked across the road from the courts. Barclay waited, and as several young school children walked home, some ventured up to the van, remaining there longer than was judged needed, just to be served ice cream.

Sensing things weren't quite right, Barclay picked his moment and fronted the driver, who seemed to quickly hide something beneath the window. The angry coach leant over and grabbed the driver by the scruff of the neck.

Fuming, he told the vendor to turn his van around, get out of the area and never show his face around the club again or he would take matters into his own hands.

Ian with top Heatherdale junior Mark Hartnett

Two young 11-year-old boys stood out among the growing numbers. Their names were Mark Hartnett and Warren Brennan. Quiet and unassuming, left-handed Hartnett was very talented and Brennan physically strong, for two boys so young.

To date, they had already produced some fine tournament results, reaching several metropolitan finals, often playing underage and often playing off against each other either in semi-finals or for trophies.

Hartnett attended St Kevin's College, located close to the inner city. Each Wednesday he would catch the train after school to attend the hitting session that Barclay ran at East Malvern in addition to his lessons at Heatherdale. Both boys continued improvement and results under Barclay only helped enhance the coach's growing reputation.

In 1975, Ian and Jackie decided to extend their business further. They opened a retail tennis shop in the neighbouring suburb of Ringwood. Called *Ian Barclay's World of Tennis*, the shop operated for six years and sold all types of racquet sports equipment, clothing and shoes. There was a restringing machine which Roy used to repair club members' racquets. Students of Ian were often employed as assistants to work in the shop.

One of Spalding's sales reps who regularly visited Barclay's shop was Jack Noseda. He had been a top-level state squash player, ranked as high as number four in Victoria. He played alongside Australian legend Geoff Hunt in the 1968

Victorian state team. He had not long returned to the squash court after a period out of the game.

Noseda encouraged Barclay an accomplished squash player himself, to have a practice hit. The two began hitting at the Brian Boys owned Squash Centre in Balwyn each Friday.

Kooyong Lawn Tennis Club's squash courts were an attraction for numerous top Victorian pennant tennis players. Some contemporaries of Barclay who combined the two sports included Will Coghlan, Colin Stubbs, Ron McKenzie, Lou Dundas and John Fraser.

They joined Barclay, Noseda and Paul Vear to form a state two pennant side. The team played together for several seasons. Noseda recalled, "Barkers exhibited great touch. He kept the ball close to the wall, moved and volleyed well, all important components one needed to bring to the squash court. He was a very good player in an era when state grade squash was extremely competitive and when there were plenty of centres in and around Melbourne." Squash nights were often long, not only on court but after the match as well.

Discussion would invariably centre on horse racing. Noseda was amazed at Barclay's knowledge of the industry. "He knew which horse had run fourth at some obscure country meeting three weeks before." Barclay's squash mates nicknamed him Custer, after the legendary American war hero General Custer, with his flowing white mane of hair. He often made his way home from squash nights late into the evening or even early into morning.

During the 1970s, local shops and centres closed at 1 pm on the weekends. That meant entire families got involved in playing sports across the two days. Barclay reflected on how many young children were therefore off the streets and put into a healthy, active environment. "Everyone's weekend was taken up with tennis, cricket or football. These days, unfortunately, at times the local shopping centres have sadly become the gathering place of many of our young who at times find themselves involved in not such healthy pastimes."

In Demand

To help ease the burden on his growing coaching numbers, Barclay took the step of forming an advanced junior hitting squad to complement his junior group classes and private lessons. The new squad started up on Wednesday afternoons, which saw Barclay cease his coaching tenure at East Malvern. Promising local juniors Anne and Elizabeth Minter from Box Hill arrived, as did others such as Rohan Goetzke, Mark Hargreaves, Joanna Meagher, Natalie McColl, Philip Ragg, Peter Beare and Gavin Jones. Players finished school then headed to the courts where their work began again. They were spread across four courts, hitting and rotating partners until they got to Mr B's court.

The increasing numbers participating in both coaching and competitions at Heatherdale gradually resulted in a strain on the supply of tennis courts. It reached a point where it had over 35 junior and senior teams competing each Saturday. Barclay's waiting list for coaching continued to grow. Heatherdale built its final two courts in 1976 to make a total of eight, thus easing the pressure on both growth areas.

One young 11-year-old boy to emerge was from North Ringwood. His name was Patrick Cash. He had been introduced to Barclay by Warren Brennan, both boys attending Whitefriars Catholic School in nearby Donvale. Barclay made the boys hit against the girls. Said Cash, "I didn't like it but he told me they could all out-rally me and he was damn right." Anne Minter, one of Barclay's more advanced juniors, was totally dedicated to improving her tennis and her strong work ethic made her a role model for the others. Soon other promising juniors, Lisa Keller and Daniel Carroll, and Wes Horskins who resided on the opposite side of town, also joined.

It wasn't long before the Barclay house became a home away from home for the local tennis fraternity. At times, it resembled a madhouse. Brothers Dean and Brad would generally have a spat with each other, which was followed by Jackie chasing them both around the house with a wooden spoon. "The greatest thing about being around the Barclay household was that the door was always open," said Cash. "Everybody was welcome and the house had a revolving door of students, club members and friends. There were tennis shoes lined up at the front door, often with only half belonging to the family. There was en tout cas dust lying everywhere. Dean and I would be playing table tennis out the back and then all of a sudden four more students or family friends would converge on the house. Jackie worked overtime keeping an eye on everyone."

Barclay believed playing singles was paramount to educating young players to think for themselves and develop more broadly. Along with junior convenor Geoff Spruzen they began to strongly lobby other nearby clubs and members of the local Association's central committee, the idea of implementing singles into what was traditionally a doubles and mixed doubles only competition. As things moved slowly, the two men created an unofficial pilot scheme that enabled the best under 14 and 16 age players from six clubs to play against each other in a singles only, after school twilight competition, held during daylight saving hours. Two boys and two girls made up a team and they each played a best of three sets match using the 12-point tie-break system. The clubs involved were Heatherdale, Donvale, Ringwood, Blackburn, East Burwood and Blackburn South.

Barclay's life was full on, with coaching, playing both pennant tennis and squash, helping Jackie raise a young family and leading an active social life all somehow running concurrently. Every Sunday following a full morning of coaching, he would load up the car with the likes of son Dean, Pat Cash, Mark Hartnett and Warren Brennan and head off to Albert Reserve in the city where the young boys would watch their coach's 'A' Grade pennant tennis match. They would then play kick-to-kick football on the cricket ground next door. If Barclay wasn't playing his own rubber, he made a point of sitting down to watch and analyse his other team mates in action. He won his second pennant with MCC in 1976. Invariably it was the team's doubles success which got them across the line in the finals.

Will Coghlan coached at the Legend Park Tennis Club in the nearby Waverley area. He and Barclay periodically conducted junior clinics together.

It hit Coghlan early on how passionate and enthusiastic Barclay was about his coaching. "Ian would try so hard to improve each pupil's strokes at our clinics, that his attitude became infectious. Analysing and then properly correcting poor technique was the major part of his mantra. He believed working with his students was like building a house.

Ian with contemporary MCC Pennant teammate and fellow coach, Will Coghlan

"They needed the strongest foundations possible in order to construct the rest of their games. If the strokes were good, they could become good players. He was adamant that you had to get the basics right." Coghlan found his own level of enthusiasm lift, simply by working alongside his mate. So focused was Barclay on producing good players, he avoided the lure of growing his business and establishing his name at multiple tennis clubs. He believed there was no point if he could not be there in person to coach.

Heatherdale Club President, Alan Bray, had his two children coached by Barclay for several years. Said Bray, "Barkers watched all his students play in the Saturday junior competition week in and week out. He followed their progress, whether they were in the highest or the lowest sections. He knew every child by name, and if not, by a nickname he had given them. If he were at a junior tournament, Barclay would make a point of spending some time watching a student's next opponent in action. His own students' parents got confused and occasionally cranky, not understanding the coach's intent, that being to pass on any helpful tips for their child's next match."

For one so young, Pat Cash impressed his coach no end, particularly with his athletic ability, strong competitive streak and great desire to be the best he could be. His groundstrokes were particularly strong from the baseline. Barclay saw no need to rush his development, but knew he would need plenty of work on his all-round game, as his volley and smash were well behind the level of his groundstrokes. Taking Barclay by surprise one day during a private lesson, the boy looked up to his coach and asked directly, "Do you think I can win Wimbledon one day, Mr B? Will you stick with me all the way?" To which Barclay replied, "Yes, I think it is possible that you can win Wimbledon, but it's a long road there and it's a lot of work, but of course I will stick with you."

Cash wanted to be better than everybody else, but needed to be harnessed somewhat, keen to achieve everything at once. He also possessed a hot temper, possibly in part due to his Irish heritage. Barclay knew there would be some ups and downs along the way with the young player's development. Cash was also a top junior Australian Rules full forward. He played for the Kew Rovers Junior Football Club and at 11 years of age had been offered a scholarship to play football with the prestigious private school, Xavier College. Cash's father Patrick Senior and his uncle Bryan had both played senior football for Hawthorn in the rough and tumble days of the 1950s, which may have said something about his sporting pedigree.

Both Mark Hartnett and Pat Cash were not that tall. When the young 12- and 11-year-olds started to play some doubles together, Barclay joked that he could drive a semi-trailer down their sidelines, as there was so much room either side of the pair. As his youngsters improved, Barclay had them play more tournaments. They played in the strong, well-established Glen Iris, Dendy Park and the December

Victorian Schoolboys' and Schoolgirls' Championships, held at Kooyong. Hartnett won the Under 13 Years Schoolboys' Singles and subsequently led the end of year CBA (Commonwealth Bank of Australia) state points' rankings race.

Warren Brennan's family then moved to Sydney for his father Terry's work. Naturally keen to maintain a close connection, the Brennans offered up their house to Barclay any time he was in the northern state with his juniors. Taking up the generous invitation, Barclay drove the family car up the highway with Hartnett, Cash, Rohan Goetzke, Wes Horskins and others on board together with a load of tennis gear, to play in the end-of-year national titles held at White City. Several others from his squad also travelled up independently. Both Hartnett and Anne Minter won their age group singles, the pair thus starting a significant run of national age title victories.

It was not uncommon for up to 10 players to stay at the Brennan's Killarney Heights house during Barclay's visits interstate. After a full day's tennis during the typically hot January school holidays, the family swimming pool back at the house was the place everyone fought to get into first. The juniors bunked down in the garage nightly for a well-earned sleep. One year, they were caught out. Some prolonged Sydney heat made way for one of the city's worst thunderstorms. Water inundated the garage and all ended up floating around the garage floor on their inflatable mattresses.

New South Wales girl Bernadette Randall came across Barclay during one of his Sydney trips. Barclay took note of Randall's unique swing on her forehand drive, the grip she used and the power she was able to generate on the shot. Her game impressed him. It wasn't long before she too jumped on board the Barclay coaching bandwagon. "Mr B saw in me the player I was. I hit the ball with my individual swing style. He didn't judge me that it wasn't constructed using textbook methods. It was what I did. I could see he could advance me to the next level with what I had. With my forehand grip though, he had to work hard to adjust it for the volley to get that shot to a better level," said Randall. The young 12-year-old went from commuting back and forward interstate each week for coaching, to living permanently at the Barclay house, thus reducing the financial burden of travelling and taking lessons. She shared a room with Toni-Ann and enrolled at the same school as both Dean and Brad – Mitcham High School. She too joined the Wednesday afternoon junior squad at Heatherdale. Promising player Sharon Hodgkin from the New South Wales border town of Albury also relocated to Melbourne to join Barclay.

Barclay's work with Pat Cash saw continued improvement in the young player's game. Said Pat, "Barkers obviously had all the best kids in Victoria. For me, it was his passion and interest in us kids, the effort he put in and his love of the game that stood out most in his character back then. Being at Heatherdale was great fun and it had a fantastic atmosphere. There were always good players around to play with. Mark Hartnett had some beautiful Dunlop Maxply wooden racquets which were imported from England and I had a couple of four by two blocks of wood, which I was always bitching about. Barkers told me when I stopped breaking my own racquets I might get the same ones as Mark.

"Barkers was always prone to some exaggeration. It was just the way he was. Rocky Loccisano and I remember one of his lessons on the serve. He demonstrated the area where the ball toss should be positioned in the court during a serve and volley exercise. I swear he was halfway to the service line, as he was that far inside the baseline. Whatever we were thinking, none of us would dare challenge him."

The Barclay house often resembled a motel. Living on the other side of Melbourne, Wes Horskins used the Barclay residence as a halfway house. He would train with the Wednesday afternoon squad, stay overnight and back it up with an early morning private lesson with his coach before returning across town and on to school. Like others, his volleys in particular took a steep learning curve.

The challenge to improve their standard of tennis meant travelling away to play more tournaments. This became a more regular occurrence for Barclay and some of his best juniors. They were often away from home for several days on end. If anyone missed their home comforts during difficult times, Ian and Jackie provided the friendly family support. Parents themselves, they could identify problems which couldn't necessarily be fixed on the tennis court.

The blue Ford Falcon Ian and Jackie owned was replaced by a new, larger gold and black Ford Fairlane that had room to fit more racquets, more balls and more kids for the tournaments they travelled to.

The historic northern Victorian town of Echuca, situated on the banks of the Murray and Campaspe Rivers held one of the state's biggest and best tournaments. Most of Barclay's top-level juniors played doubles with him at Echuca, where historically he'd had plenty of success himself. He would partner each of them and use the experience to further educate them about the game.

Kaye Wearne, Ian, Jackie and Brian Wearne

It was in Echuca, years earlier in 1955, that Barclay first met local resident Brian Wearne.

At one time in his life, Wearne held the position of Mayor of Echuca, like his father before him. He was also the President of the Tennis Club for many years and was a tireless worker on its behalf.

The two men became close friends, with Wearne proving a tower of strength for Barclay in both his playing and coaching careers.

Barclay conducted clinics on the club's pristine grass courts. Brian and his wife Kaye's generosity allowed Ian and Jackie to stay at their home on many occasions when the tournament was being held. Both sets of children became close friends.

The Heatherdale Tennis Club acknowledged the increased amount of time and commitment Barclay showed. He would spend many hours, over and above his paid hours at the club with his pupils, in search of ways to either fine-tune a serve or strengthen a groundstroke. His generous nature extended to him not leaning on some parents to pay for their children's fees when due, particularly those who were either having several lessons a week or who were under financial stress. He didn't want to turn anyone away from the game. He also spent plenty of extra time maintaining the club's courts. The shifting surface suffered somewhat through general play, but particularly during times of either heavy winter rain or strong summer winds. He was often seen with a shovel in hand, spreading new en tout cas over any number of damaged courts. It was within both his and the club's interests to have the courts in the best condition possible. This was an example of Barclay going to the nth degree.

Like Ian, Jackie played in the summer competition tennis for the club, featuring regularly in midweek ladies' fixtures and filling in for Saturday teams when needed, occasionally alongside her husband. The pairing naturally produced a competitive environment. She was a key member of the Heatherdale midweek ladies' committees, as well as the club's social committees. The ladies also sought and received coaching from Barclay. He didn't miss anyone.

At Heatherdale, his new pilot competition scheme that offered singles match play for the best local juniors ran for a second year. Its success finally prompted the Association's central committee into establishing an official combined singles and doubles competition on Saturday mornings during the 1977-78 summer season for a select number of sections.

Improvement in Barclay's best juniors brought more success. Not having won a set the previous year in Sydney, Pat Cash won the Under 13 Singles title at the interstate end-of-year national age titles. Such was the progress of Barclay's Wednesday afternoon junior squad, there were now three national age titleholders in it. Others were also well ranked in their age groups. There was a fierce desire by all to both improve and impress their coach. Barclay continued to encourage those beneath the top group to work as hard, if not harder than those ranked above them. He continually reminded all his students that they would only get out of their tennis what they were prepared to put into it.

Barclay was not frightened to seek advice from close colleague Will Coghlan in the event that he needed a second opinion on the development of any student. Said Coghlan, "Ian thought that at times four eyes were better than two in his quest to make his juniors better players and it was a privilege to be his sounding board."

Having being a one-man band at Heatherdale during his early days, demand for coaching, together with a waiting list that had ballooned out considerably, meant Barclay needed to bring an assistant coach on board. He felt that if one of his students or an outsider was genuinely interested and could cut the cloth as a coach, he would offer up the opportunity.

One such person to take on that role in the late 1970s was a young university student named Ann Quinn who lived in nearby Blackburn. Ironically, years earlier as a younger teenager, her parents couldn't get her into Barclay's coaching program because she was too far back on his waiting list. Quinn was undertaking a Human Movement Degree and during the first week of her first year was thrown in at the deep end. She and her fellow students were required to do 100 hours of fieldwork experience in the sport of their choice. Naturally, everyone chose their favourite sport.

Quinn contacted prominent people in Victorian tennis circles looking for advice on whom she might approach. Nine out of the ten she called all directed her towards Barclay. Not knowing the Heatherdale tennis coach, she rang him, explained her situation and that, if possible, he was the person she would like to work with. His simple reply was, "Sure, love, come along." Her 100 hours would go on to become five years working alongside Barclay.

She was intrigued at how easily Barclay could identify errors in a student's technique and would often ask him what he was observing in a player's strokes, as he would pick up on every minute, technical detail, which was difficult to see. She often went back to the Barclay house after the coaching day to study in slow motion the on-court video recordings of students with whom they worked. Years of doing this helped Quinn towards her own future coaching and educational work. She believed Barclay's great knack of picking up on the smallest technical deficiency was both an art and a science. "He had an incredible eye for detail and for noticing the little things. On top of that was his desire to then make corrections, in some cases spending hours on the practice court fixing whatever problems. This was a special quality. He was always upbeat and encouraging, with endless energy."

During her ongoing studies, Ann Quinn felt that with the length of time Barclay's juniors were spending at squad sessions, it would be good to look a little more into their fitness and training needs, to complement their hitting. Basic training such as warm-ups, stretching, flexibility and cooling down were slowly integrated into sessions. She gradually introduced hill sprints on the inclines adjacent to the club and agility exercises on the football oval next door. She was ever mindful that the children were there primarily to learn to play tennis, so made sure the training drills she introduced were tennis specific, and centred on speed, agility and recovery. Quinn took the best players in the squad to the university to analyse their strengths and weaknesses in much more detail. "Ian and I are both such perfectionists. For us, both individually and collectively, it was a matter of what can we do to help these young players be the very best they can? No stone was left unturned."

Another to step up to an assistant coaching role with Barclay in 1978 was Charles Kneale. He had been coaching in the Camberwell area, but was looking for a change. He also wanted to work on his own game. Kneale too was directed towards Barclay and commenced lessons on Friday mornings, immediately after young Pat Cash. A keen student of the game, he would arrive half an hour early just to observe Barclay at work with the youngster. Like Quinn, he too recognised Barclay's sharp eye for picking up the finer details in a player's game. "It wouldn't surprise me if his ability to diagnose a problem could well be a visual skill he acquired during his days as a commercial artist," said Kneale.

Barclay continued to attract young players from far and wide. Locally, Geoff and Kay Stone brought their young eight-year-old daughter, Carolyn, across from the neighbouring Blackburn South Tennis Club, primarily because of the club's short-sighted policy which didn't allow youngsters to become members till they were 10 years of age. As would be discovered later, Barclay and Kay Stone had two bizarre links. Unbeknown, they had been born on the same day, in the same hospital. Just as surprising was Kay's father had previously worked at the same company – Colourprint – at the same time as Ian.

Children from country Victoria came down for Barclay's school holiday clinics at Heatherdale. Some then stayed on for private lessons. One young boy from Echuca in northern Victoria was Andrew Crossman. Having previously experienced a clinic with Barclay in his home town, aged nine and showing promise, he was put on a bus and a train by his parents for the three-hour trip to Melbourne to have coaching once a month with Barclay. As he improved, this increased to once a week.

Barclay continued to be in demand.

Ever-supportive Father

Life for the Barclays became increasingly busy. The children spent less time with their father, as he was invariably tied up with all things tennis coaching, but he was ever supportive. "We still had everything we needed as children though," remarked Dean. "Dad was a great provider." Generally, they saw their dad first thing in the morning before school and then late at night after coaching had finished. Thursday night was the one night he finished coaching earlier than most. The children helped cook his omelette for dinner, before he hurriedly set off for his evening pennant squash match. If they were lucky, both Dean and Brad got to go with their dad on some of his squash nights.

Barclay fully supported his children's choices of sports and would do all he could to get to their respective games and see them play. Dean, the eldest child, was in the same mould as his father, a natural at all sports. He found tennis both fun and easy to pick up, but was also a very good footballer and enjoyed the team aspect of the sport more. It allowed him to play with his mates and placed him in an environment where he felt less self-imposed pressure to achieve. He played much of his formative years at the adjacent Heatherdale Junior Football Club. So talented was Dean, one year he was invited to try out with the Essendon Football Club's development squad. Ian also served a number of seasons on the local football club's committee.

Daughter Toni-Ann, at eight years of age, had been playing softball in the Under 14 Bears team, closely monitored by her mother, now an umpire at both national and international levels. She began to play tennis, so her father cut a senior length wooden racquet down in size in order to help her control the ball. The youngest of the three Barclay children, tennis for Toni-Ann was simply a social outlet. "Ironically, tennis was a low priority for me at the time, especially coming from an extremely competitive family." Very much the character brother, Brad confessed to being one of his father's worst tennis students, particularly when on the same coaching court as his father. "I was best served on another court as I was always cheeky and looking for any attention I could get from Dad."

If one was a Barclay, there was only one football team to follow and that was Hawthorn. During the season, anybody who stepped foot inside the Barclay household soon realised the fact. It took little time for an argument to start, generally over the result of a weekend match. A Hawks loss was unacceptable and everyone had an opinion. The boys accompanied their father to the club's home games at the Glenferrie Oval, as well as away games. The Ford Fairlane was regularly crammed with friends and supporters for Saturday's matches. Brad remembered one Saturday winter's afternoon when four fathers and sons crammed into the car for a match out at Waverley Park. How they never got pulled over by the police, he never knew.

On occasions, the family found time for a holiday together, particularly down at Inverloch, a popular beach resort in the South Gippsland region. It was just the norm that aunts, uncles and friends of the Barclays went along as well. Holidays were also spent on the Sunshine Coast in Queensland.

At Marcus Beach one year, tennis mate Ray O'Connor decided to paddle out through the waves on a surf mat but got caught in a rip. Seeing the incident from the family's beachside motel, Barclay dashed downstairs, dropped his gold watch on the sand alongside O'Connor's eldest daughter Kim and proceeded into the water to help his mate who he feared may get washed away. On reaching the stricken paddler, Barclay was told everything was okay and not to worry. Heading back to shore, Jackie could only identify her husband when his head bobbed up out of the water, as the mane of white hair got lost in the foamy wash. In taking a liking to Queensland, not long after they purchased a two-storey house further north in Hervey Bay.

As Toni-Ann got older, she became more serious about her own tennis. "Dad used me to practice with some of the girls who came from overseas to have coaching from him. He didn't watch many of my own tournament matches because I didn't enjoy him watching, knowing he would pick up on my mistakes. If I won, he would make sure to remind me how many double faults I served or how many forehands hit the net. It was probably the father/daughter relationship. Mum was far more encouraging." A self-confessed better doubles than singles player, Toni-Ann won her fair share of junior titles. Aged 15, she and her father won the Adelaide Hardcourt Mixed Doubles title in 1984, defeating a very young Mark Woodforde, a future Australian doubles legend.

Broader Horizons

Much of Ian Barclay's early coaching was conducted in an era when neither the Lawn Tennis Association of Australia (LTAA) nor state tennis bodies had any development programs in place for aspiring juniors. Australia's tennis greats including Frank Sedgman, Lew Hoad, Neale Fraser, Ken Rosewall, Rod Laver, Roy Emerson, John Newcombe and Tony Roche had all had been reared by private coaches. When he became a full-time professional coach, training for players for the Linton and Wilson Cup state underage teams was held at Kooyong.

In addition, the development and success Barclay had achieved with his group of young juniors to date seemed to draw a degree of jealousy and resentment from within the state's coaching establishment, the Tennis Coaches Association of Victoria (TCAV – previously PTAV). It appeared that a number of senior coaches had some identity problems, reflective of the perceived closed shop approach to those on the outside like Barclay, who were not members, and not regarded as particularly good players. Barclay didn't agree with elements of the coaching guidelines set by the TCAV and was apt to make his feelings known. As a result, he was continually reminded by some in perceived higher places that he would never make a real player out of his best pupils, in particular Pat Cash. Ironically, he was failed when attempting to pass his first coaching exam. The running joke at the Kooyong Tennis Club was that the association failed him on his best stroke, his backhand volley.

The following year John Newcombe began to run his Custom Credit sponsored junior squads in both Sydney and around New South Wales. Not having a particularly high regard for Barclay's coaching abilities either, Newcombe thought he should have the pick of all the good young players from around the country, including Cash. The youngster wasn't interested in going interstate and joining Newcombe, much happier to stay loyal and develop his game under Barclay's guidance back at Heatherdale. The rejection resulted in one rather distasteful newspaper article written about Barclay and some further subsequent belittling of Cash by Newcombe and his ghostwriters within the print media.

Barclay continually encouraged his charges to work hard. In 1979, Hartnett, Cash and Anne Minter yet again won their national age group singles titles. The questions soon came from those close to him. What was his next move? Barclay realised he needed to get his best juniors out of their comfort zone. The next move had to be trying their hand overseas against the world's best. That would mean taking children thousands of kilometres away from home and at considerable cost.

With no finance or assistance available through the LTAA, Barclay had to go it alone and look elsewhere for help. He began to network the idea around his close circles. A group of businessmen and identities were targeted and a number got involved, including well-known Australian rock music and event entrepreneur Michael Edgley, who became a primary financier. Others from diverse business backgrounds helped underwrite the venture. Pat Cash's father, Patrick Senior, and his Uncle Leo attended to legal and administrative matters. A new organisation called *Make a Tennis Champion Here* (MATCH) emerged.

The Heatherdale Tennis Club's General Committee embraced Barclay's desire to go abroad. Assistant coaches Ann Quinn and Charles Kneale were charged with running the junior coaching program in his absence.

Such was Barclay's professionalism, he left giving Quinn and Kneale an outline on every student's requirements. "It was a list of every stroke for all 350 kids he coached and the teaching points we needed to emphasise for each stroke for each of those players. It was pages and pages long. Such was the nth degree he would go to even for the youngest of his charges and beginner level players," said Quinn.

Kneale quizzed his mentor on what might happen if either assistant wasn't well enough to attend a night's coaching. He was promptly told the only time a coach shouldn't turn up for work was if they were in a box. Kneale got the hint.

Ian with the First MATCH team
Mark Hartnett, Pat Cash, Wally Masur,
Elizabeth and Anne Minter

With Ian and wife Jackie at the helm, the first MATCH junior team consisted of Mark Hartnett, Patrick Cash, Wally Masur (from Canberra) Anne Minter and younger sister Elizabeth.

The Minter sisters' parents had already given their daughters an opportunity to play overseas, previously embarking on two private trips to Europe. The experience gave them a good insight into the challenges that lay ahead.

The team arrived on European shores in early 1979 for a six-week tour, which included competing in the prestigious Avvenire Cup held in Milano, Italy.

Jackie looked after the meals, administration and most of the organisation of the team.

The girls enjoyed having her close by. The study she had done of the Italian language beforehand helped them navigate their way around.

Of the young touring players, she demanded good manners and proper etiquette wherever they went. Said Cash, "In many ways, Jackie was the glue that held our first trip together."

Jackie and Ian pictured in Milan in 1979. A perfect match, born out of love, respect and a mutual desire to help to develop junior tennis

In their new foreign tennis domain, the young Australians found the going tough. Albeit having some good doubles performances, the team predominantly struggled in the singles.

They found the clay courts played significantly slower and the balls bounced higher in comparison to what they were used to back in Melbourne.

The Europeans were supremely fit, organised, well managed and knew the art of playing on clay courts. Along with the South Americans, many used extreme western grips on the forehand side, which increased their topspin. At the same time, they could also generate great power off the ultra-slow surface. The Swedes' style of play mirrored their multi-winning Grand Slam champion Bjorn Borg.

Some of the names in the main draw included future champions such as Swede Stefan Edberg, Czechoslovak Miloslav Mecir and French boy Guy Forget. Previous winners of the Avvenire Cup were the likes of Czech players Ivan Lendl and Hana Mandlikova and Swedish all-time great Borg. Pat Cash was fortunate enough to practice with a young Swede called Mats Wilander, who Barclay said "did not miss a ball".

The young MATCH group returned back to Australia with a different mindset. So did their coach. While in Europe they were made plainly aware by Barclay that although they were talented, they would need to work that much harder in order to make any realistic inroads on the international stage, particularly when playing on clay. Two things were at the forefront of the coach's mind for his players' development. Firstly, they needed an unbreakable competitive spirit. Secondly, they needed to learn to defend the court as well as their European counterparts. He felt it was imperative that their defence was the equal of their offence. They also needed to work on methods to become fitter. In Europe they had run out of steam while their opponents had marched on.

Back on home soil, work began straight away again at Heatherdale. Barclay made subtle changes to training on Wednesday squad nights and in his private lessons. His juniors needed to learn to hit the ball higher across the net when in defensive positions, so he either wound the nets up higher or repositioned the singles sticks. Barclay proceeded to send young Pat Cash off to pennant team mate Dr John Fraser for some early morning training sessions before school, to help with his endurance.

Barclay also penned his first newspaper article concerning court surfaces. He believed that Australian tennis authorities needed to invest in and lay down European-style clay courts as quickly as possible. He was convinced that because of the speed and bounce of the ball, it was the best surface on which to train and help juniors develop their games. Just as importantly, this was the predominant surface the best juniors in the world were playing on, so if Aussies at large were going to make any impact on the world stage, the introduction of a clay surface at home was imperative.

The continued hard work at Heatherdale paid off substantially as Anne Minter then won the Australian Open Girls' Singles in December, defeating West Australian Elizabeth Sayers in the final 6-4, 6-2. Bernadette Randall, aged just 14 years, also performed strongly, winning three State Under 16 Junior titles in Victoria, New South Wales and Queensland. Both girls thrilled Barclay as they then got a taste of tennis at the highest level by playing in the main draw of the Australian Open Women's Singles for the first time.

Barclay increased his networking. He and Adelaide coach Jan MacDonald first met in Sydney at the Linton, Wilson and Reid Cups junior State Teams Carnival in 1980, both in roles as team coaches. Barclay had Hartnett, Cash, Anne Minter, Horskins, Randall and Hodgkin all competing at various stages in representative teams for their state. During her own junior playing days, MacDonald competed in the Wilson Cup team for South Australia and was highly ranked in her home state. Her own coach at the time, Tom Joy, had a reciprocal arrangement with leading Melbourne coach, Keith Rogers. They took their top juniors back and forward each year to the other's state to play in tournaments and stay with opposing players and their families.

In only her second trip away, aged 16, MacDonald played in the Australian Hardcourt title and stayed and trained with one of Rogers' protégés, an 18-year-old called Margaret Smith (later Court). Believing she was fit, MacDonald joined in a training session with Smith. This involved a run to another Victorian girl, Kerry Melville's home, some five kilometres away. It was to be followed by a two-hour gymnasium session. With the run and gym session over, a fatigued MacDonald was ready to call it quits and wondered who was coming to pick both girls up to take them home. A superbly fit Smith had other ideas and they ran home. MacDonald had the misfortune to later play Smith in two successive Australian Opens. Like Barclay, MacDonald didn't travel overseas, but played the national circuit. Once the grind of playing took its toll, MacDonald remained in Adelaide and found herself helping out her old coach, Joy. That progressed to her taking on and teaching her own students.

As the national carnival progressed, the two effervescent coaches got on well. As it happened, coaches and teams from both states stayed in the same hotel in Sydney's inner Kings Cross. Each evening after the day's play, the adults headed across the road to a hotel to relax over a few drinks and whatever light entertainment was on offer. Every hour someone went back to the hotel to check on their sleeping team members. The bond between the two camps grew, so much so that afterwards they generally ended up late into the night in one hotel room drinking coffee and sharing tennis yarns, often in their pyjamas. MacDonald invited Barclay to bring over a group of juniors to South Australia for their own private challenge. Noting her wonderful personality and relationship with her own players, he jumped at the chance.

Andrew Crossman recalled the first trip Barclay's squad took across the border. "We took a bus with about twenty 10-16 year olds and were due to arrive at the MacDonald's house around 5 pm the same day. However, courtesy of four flat tyres and a flat battery, we were never going to get there on time. We spent much of the day and night stuck on the side of the highway waiting for repairs to arrive. It was one of the only times I can remember Barkers ever really losing his cool." Meanwhile Jan MacDonald's students and their parents had arrived hours earlier at her house in suburban Highgate, in anticipation of the Victorians' arrival, eager for their new experience to begin. At 1 am the following morning, Barclay and his team finally arrived in Adelaide. Relieved, but still angry, Barclay duly gave the major bus company a piece of his mind, for allowing what he considered to be a totally unroadworthy vehicle to carry children, or for that matter anyone on such a long journey.

Tired, but raring to go, players took to the courts the following day for their challenge match at the Roselands Tennis Centre in the Adelaide suburb of Marion, where McDonald worked as the Head Coach. Barclay felt the biggest challenge for his players was to get a fresh look at someone they had never played before and have to think for themselves, without any help. Here was that opportunity. Every player played multiple singles, doubles and mixed doubles matches. The plan was to get as much tennis into the day as possible.

Both coaches didn't just invite their best players to their challenges. Children of parents who held committee positions or who were outstanding club members and volunteers at the respective clubs were also given an opportunity to travel. Both Barclay and MacDonald realised the importance of all those connected to grassroots tennis and felt no area should be ignored. It was also important to give as many players as possible both tennis and other life experiences. The chance to live away from home, build one's communication skills, use good manners and work within a team were at times a challenge but created invaluable lessons. Here again was Barclay going to the nth degree.

In a traditionally individual sport, the travel experience created the dynamic of a big family. All this was of far greater interest to both coaches, at the expense of making any significant financial return for themselves. They didn't care. They only wanted to make their students better players and better people. MacDonald attributed the quality of Barclay's caring character that parents from his tennis club put such trust in him to take care of their children.

With each day's tennis over, players dispersed to their respective host families. Barclay sat back with MacDonald and her architect husband Ian over a glass of the iconic Barossa Valley's finest red wine. They chewed the fat and dissected the day's play into the deep hours. Then it was back again the next day for another full day of tennis. Every second year it was the other's turn to host the challenge. Friendships were made, some of which remain decades on.

Barclay and his best juniors returned to MacDonald's house when other major tournaments were held in Adelaide, particularly during October for the annual long weekend BP (British Petroleum) sponsored tournament, held at the East Torrens Kensington Gardens Tennis Club. One year, 27 people stayed at her house. Players filled the swimming pool after each day's tennis. The backyard tennis court was used if extra practice was needed. Barclay amazed MacDonald. "He was in many ways just one of the kids, into everything that was going. He was willing to sleep anywhere in the house if there were no spare beds, wash dishes and help cook the nightly barbecue. He didn't need a five-star hotel. He had breakfast with all the kids in the morning and had a million laughs with each of them. One night did get a bit scary though. Barkers had the heat on the barbecue turned up very high. Unaware, he had allowed an excessive amount of fat to remain on the hotplate. Flames suddenly engulfed the cooking food and surrounds, then shot up and burned all my plants hanging from the roof of the pergola."

MacDonald and her junior squad, which included her two children Melissa and Alistair, returned to the Heatherdale Tennis Club every second year. They had to contend with Victoria's traditional en tout cas surface. Brought up on hard courts in their home state, the travellers often ended up on their rear ends, having struggled with the vagaries of the slippery surface, much to the laughter of their coaches. They learned the hard way, the subtle nuances of having to slide into shots and then recover for the next. They were also not used to sweeping a tennis court after every set. Back at the Barclay household, Jackie cooked meals for their interstate friends, as always, with a big smile on her face. The Barclay family graciously opened the door to their South Australian friends year after year, particularly during school holiday tournaments.

The second MATCH trip in 1980 gave Barclay a better insight into his juniors' progress. The team again comprised Mark Hartnett, Pat Cash, Anne and Elizabeth Minter with new players from his squad, Bernadette Randall and Sharon Hodgkin joining the team.

Just prior to her first European experience, Randall slipped on a court line while doing a running exercise, fell and broke her left wrist. Before leaving, Hartnett's father John, a doctor, carefully fitted a plaster cast on her hand that allowed her to toss the ball up in the air on serve with relative comfort.

If there was an omen, Jackie Barclay set the scene by deciding she wanted to take the team to the Vatican in Rome, where Pope John II was due to ordain a new priest inside St Peter's Church.

The team had a sprinkling of Catholics in its ranks, so Jackie wanted to make the most of the opportunity. She was stunned at the mass of people lined up en route to the church. On being ushered towards the front of the crowd, the tennis group waited patiently. Soon after the Pope arrived, leading the ceremony. Out of nowhere, he quietly stepped off the red carpet, went across to Ian and gave him a blessing. Jackie nearly fainted.

Ironically, the self-confessed atheist jokingly whispered to his team that was all they needed to win the Avvenire Cup. In the city renowned for pickpockets, the warning had gone out to everyone to keep their hands on any valuables. They felt blessed yet again when by accident, Hartnett dropped his wallet in the street. By some miracle, a local vendor approached the group and kindly returned it, untouched.

The young Barclay children – Dean, Brad and Toni-Ann – remained in Australia with family and friends while their mother and father were away overseas. At times, it could be for as long as three months. It was sometimes difficult to cope but the children were normally used to having lots of people around the home. Over time, they adjusted very well. Mindful of the high cost of overseas calls, the children received a telephone call once a week from Ian and Jackie to catch up on news at both ends. All three were guaranteed plenty of presents on their parents' return.

To mark the team's improvement, a year from the previous year, an outstanding performance by Hartnett saw him win the coveted Avvenire Cup's 16 and Under Boys' Singles title. In the company of some of the world's best juniors, he defeated French boy Tarik Benhabiles in the final. The silky left-hander regularly used short and deep angles to push the French junior wide off the court, thereby opening up space to put away his dominant groundstrokes and volleys. Being left-handed, he was typically hard to pick, often taking his opponent by surprise by going back behind him with accurate sliced backhands. He maintained a high percentage of accurate first serves, thus keeping pressure on his opponent's returns. He complemented his natural attacking game with a considerably improved defence, an area which had been hammered into the team by Barclay on the back of their previous tour. Hartnett's win also secured the team trophy for the Australians.

However, in victory Hartnett also suffered an injury to his back. On waking up the day after the singles final, he was in pain, barely able to move. Hartnett and Cash were due to play the doubles final against Benhabiles and his French team mate Loic Courteau.

Both Aussie boys had continued to develop into a formidable team back home. Having both grown, the left- and right-handed combination complemented each other in all areas. Other teams had struggled to pass them when they were both at the net. At times in tournaments the boys would fool around in front of their coach, just to test him out, but if he turned away, in no time they would win three or four games on the trot and follow it up with a cheeky look across to Barclay that said "We told you we would be okay, Mr B." The boys had grasped Barclay's teaching of the doubles game well, to the point where they had won every doubles tournament they played together in.

Although getting up for the match, Hartnett could only move freely to one side. Barclay instructed the boys to play the tandem formation on serve, so as to help protect his restricted movement. Cash's form was good, as he had won two lead-up junior singles titles in Bologna and Bari. But it was his performance with

Hartnett in the doubles final that left an indelible mark in the coach's mind. Such was Cash's dominant performance, Barclay now realised just what a fierce competitor he had. Cash confidently remarked to his coach that like Hartnett the following year he would come back and win the Avvenire Singles title. Barclay told his young charge, who was a year younger than the other competitors in the field, that it was a great attitude but he would need to put in a substantial amount of work to fulfil his ambition. Cash replied, "Don't you worry about that, Mr B, I'll do it."

Barclay quietly confided in Jackie that he believed the young protégé had the potential to win something special one day. Added salt was given to this thought as Cash won the Under 16 Singles title at the German Junior Championships in Berlin.

The girls also featured more prominently another year on. Sharon Hodgkin won the Under 16 Singles titles in Berlin and also in Livorno, Italy. Bernadette Randall also won the Under 16 Single s title in Bologna.

It wasn't uncommon for an overly eager parent to want to gain an edge by trying to intimidate the young Australians from outside the court. Jackie was on hand and stepped in. Enough said.

One of Barclay's other Heatherdale students, Wes Horskins, who was not a part of the MATCH team, had linked up with another independent touring team from Sydney.

The two group's itineraries inadvertently overlapped for a couple of weeks in Europe, allowing Horskins to spend some time with his fellow Heatherdale friends. The promising Horskins took out two titles – the Swiss National Junior Singles title in Landquart as well as the Czechoslovakian Junior Championships (Slovakia).

Towards the conclusion of the 1980 trip, the team played a tournament in the town of Klosters in Switzerland. Hodgkin again won an Under 16 Singles title. It was here that Cash beat Hartnett for the first time in singles. Barclay had told his two boys it wasn't fair for him to give any tips to either so they were on their own in the final, the coach determined to stay impartial. The team stayed in a rather plush hotel that the Swiss Royalty often used on their holidays. The boys couldn't help but get up to some mischief away from the tennis court. They managed to get their hands on some fireworks and set them off in the girls' rooms. Unbeknown to them, the female owner of the hotel was an ex-war widow. She became increasingly agitated over the noise of the successive explosions. It gave her horrible flashbacks to earlier years. The boys knew they were in trouble. "Jackie got hold of Mark and me and gave us a huge dressing-down. We had to apologise profusely to the lady," said Cash.

After a scan was conducted on Hartnett's back, the injury turned out to be a stress fracture of the L5 vertebrae. Barclay feared what the injury could do to his elite player's future tennis aspirations. He took 12 months off tennis and concentrated on finishing his secondary schooling. Cash played pennant tennis in a 'B Special' team at Grace Park Tennis Club, with some 'A' Grade matches thrown in against experienced players, some not long off the professional tour.

The two European trips to date had been an invaluable experience for Barclay's juniors.

After her second MATCH trip away, Anne Minter decided to leave the coach's stable. Minter had been one of Barclay's hardest workers and most dedicated players. Her tennis continued to improve. She won the Italian Open Girls' Singles, gained an ITF world junior ranking of number two, and then won the Australian Open Girls' Singles twice again. Minter also won the 1980 Australian Open Girls' Doubles with Victorian girl Miranda Yates. She proceeded to travel on her own for the next five years on the Women's Tennis Association (WTA) professional tour.

Her next coach, Melbourne's Graham Harris, travelled with her extensively and eventually they married. She went on to win four titles, reached the Canadian Open semi-final with a win against legend Chris Evert, and made the fourth round at Wimbledon twice. Her best result came with a quarter-final appearance at the 1988 Australian Open at Melbourne Park. Minter attained a career-high ranking of 23. She and husband coach Harris often bumped into Barclay at the Grand Slam events, the coach continuing to keep an interest in his former pupil's game.

In 1981, the LTAA finally succumbed to pressure that had been indirectly applied to it by the success of Barclay's MATCH team's results the previous year. Together with leading business, National Panasonic, the Association came on board, lending financial assistance to Barclay's project. Ironically, it also took over the naming rights.

The team included the experienced Cash, Randall and Elizabeth Minter and was now joined by new players John Frawley from Queensland, Jamie Harty from New South Wales, and South Australian, Natalia Leipus. It was about to face by far its strongest overseas opposition yet. The team played six tournaments in one and a half months.

Minter won the Under 16 Singles title and Randall the Under 18 title at the German Junior Championships held in Moenchengladbach. Randall yet again won the Under 16 Singles in Bologna, this time defeating Minter in the final. Meanwhile Cash won the Under 18 Singles title in Bari, before the Australian team yet again contested the Avvenire Cup in Milano. The quarter-final list of boys that contested the main singles event was outstanding. These included France's Guy Forget, Czechoslovak Karel Novacek, Spaniard Emilio Sanchez, and Swede Stefan Edberg. It was the toughest field Barclay had seen. All eight would eventually go on to reach top 10 rankings on the Men's professional tour.

Barclay's new number one spearhead, Cash took all before him, having clearly learned how to play on the clay courts. Moving through the draw, he had more power in his shots than the other players. Barclay felt he played his best tennis in the quarter-final where he defeated Sanchez in an epic three-set encounter. From then on he was relentless, accounting for Novacek in the semi-final. He played Edberg in the final, who at that time was still using a double-hand backhand. Having played on the forehand side in doubles with Mark Hartnett, his cross-court forehand was deadly accurate. His finishing shots were precise. He won the final relatively easily, ensuring the team successfully defended the teams' title. Yet again, Cash had doubles success, teaming up with Harty to win the Boys' title.

Barclay's thoughts were further strengthened, that in Cash Australia definitely had a potential Grand Slam title winner.

With the Avvenire Cup secure in Australian hands, the team continued touring and played several more tournaments. Typical of Ian's and Jackie's compassion, they took on and looked after young Spaniard Sanchez when the manager of the Spanish junior team became ill. For Bernadette Randall, the European clay became her favourite surface. The slow, high bounce clearly suited her game. Buoyed by her results, she wanted to continue playing in Europe, but faced the financial and educational realities of life and had to return home and head back to school.

Barclay was eternally indebted to those who underwrote the MATCH project. Initially after the 1979 trip, he feared after only limited success those financing the syndicate might think it was a forlorn exercise and that those juniors may only ever succeed locally. But, fortunately, they too must have seen light at the end of the tunnel, for they continued to inject the necessary funds to send Barclay's juniors away again and the second year's performances started to justify the outlay. After the 1981 junior tour, Barclay felt his charges were still in the teething stages of catching up with the rest of the world. He felt they needed the same level of competition eight months of the year to make any real impact. The benefits, however, would continue to play out significantly in the years to come.

Barclay wasn't the only one tough on his juniors. Wife Jackie could be even tougher. She was quite single-minded as to where she thought the tennis partnership with her husband should go and was fully behind the formation of the MATCH concept. Her previous involvement at the elite level of softball had her well grounded for the many challenges that lay ahead in the cut-throat world of competitive tennis. She was a driving force when the juniors travelled. She needed a certain amount of hardness about her in order to help them make breakthroughs on the world stage, but could just as easily find compassion when it was needed. She made a wise decision to learn several foreign languages over time to help breakdown some of the communication barriers. She was adamant that those around her used correct grammar when they spoke.

Pat Cash suggested the MATCH project helped kickstart junior development in Australia. "Getting results overseas embarrassed the LTAA into doing something about junior tennis. It's hard to believe there was barely anything happening back then. There were no official junior development programs in place for anyone under the age of 18 years."

Those in Barclay's Heatherdale junior squad who had not been overseas realised the amount and level of work put in by those who had. Very few who went on one of Barclay's overseas trips were not national titleholders. He believed that if you weren't a national champion, your chances of success overseas at the highest level were almost impossible and you probably shouldn't go. He still holds the same belief strongly today, even more so as the number of countries playing tennis and the depth of talent in the sport has increased so much. Les Petits As in Tarbes, one of, if not Europe's biggest Junior 14 and Under tournaments held in France, had a 64 draw full of national champions from each country when the MATCH team toured. Its honour board suggested the historic winners of the tournament generally went on to have successful careers in the game.

Back at Heatherdale

Barclay returned after each trip away and went straight back to work at Heatherdale. He would step off a plane, play in a local pennant match if required, or go off to a junior tournament to observe more matches, such was his devotion to the club and his kids. Whatever issues he encountered back at the club, his demeanour never changed. He always attended its social functions.

Jackie often joked that the only time the business ever made any money was when Ian was away and his assistant coaches ran it on their behalf.

Barclay readily made himself available to play in the association's Saturday afternoon summer senior competition. Heatherdale, like many clubs at the time, had long held a policy that juniors played competition on Saturdays mornings and seniors in the afternoons, albeit with some exceptions. He wanted his best juniors to play alongside him in the club's highest section. Granted the coach's continued development with his students, the club further loosened its policy and granted the coach his wish.

Just like with his trips to Echuca, Barclay knew that his teaching would be best realised if the youngsters he was guiding were on court with him week in and week out when the pressure was on to perform. In backing himself and his charges, Barclay promised premiership flags and duly delivered.

Teaming up with young Cash, Hartnett, Randall and Hodgkin in Section 1, they often inflicted some severe losses on opposing clubs. He would often come across opposition team captains who would corner him after a heavy loss and lambaste him, "Barkers, don't you ever bring those bloody kids back here again." Heatherdale's arch rival during those days was the Donvale Tennis Club. Barclay chuckled when reliving one match when he and his youngsters had a day out as they went up 24 games to nil after the first four sets, effectively killing off the match, much to the chagrin of the opposition.

Barclay led by example, consistently executing a high percentage of first serves and service returns, particularly when it mattered most in sets. He backed it up with sharp movement around the court and pinpoint execution of his volleys. He had a canny ability to read the play and be a split second ahead of everyone else on the court. He could quickly identify a weakness in an opponent and expose it under pressure.

He would often use his favourite tactic of playing the ball behind an opponent during rallies to either win the point outright or set up an easy volley or smash for himself or his young partner. He made the education of the game simple for his pupils and kept crucial words close at hand for the times when the kids he partnered needed to hear them most: "Make sure you get your first serve in, don't let the lob get over your head, keep the ball over the net at all costs, keep moving forward, don't hit the million-to-one shot." The juniors, and even adult partners (like Noel McMahon back in the early Echuca days), came to hear these clichés over and over again, week in and week out. However frustrating it could be at times for his charges, it fostered a great level of respect and trust in Barclay and his knowledge of what was required to play consistent competitive tennis.

During the summer competition season he would join the horde of other club players for after-match drinks at the local Manhattan Hotel, situated a short walk from the club. Given his tendency to sometimes exaggerate his tennis stories, Barclay was often the butt of a joke from club members, but loved it and gave plenty back in good spirit.

Two more students arrived to have coaching with Barclay in 1980. They were local boys Martin Kozma and Rocky Loccisano.

Like Charles Kneale before him, Kozma too had decided to take up some private lessons to improve his game. He encountered a huge level of energy on his first venture down to the back courts at Heatherdale "Pupils were being guided using Barkers' black and white teaching formula. They either did it the correct way or they struggled to do it at all. There was no room for grey areas." Similar to those before him, Barclay's charisma, enthusiasm and magnetism blew Kozma away and it instantly drew him towards the coach. Although confessing to be one of the least gifted technically and one of the oldest in his group, Kozma knew this was the scene for him and like Kneale and Ann Quinn before him, took on board everything Barclay taught him. Even from his first 45-minute lesson, Kozma saw the vision regarding what was required both technically and tactically to be a good tennis player. He was amazed at the volume of young players practising, having private lessons and the level of commitment demonstrated. He decided to offer himself up for any jobs Barclay needed done, such as hanging around to be a hitting partner if required; anything to enhance his knowledge and thirst for improvement. A year after commencing lessons, Kozma was offered an assistant coaching role.

Loccisano, aged 15, commenced with private lessons and then joined the Wednesday squad the following year. On Barclay he said, "Barkers' lesson plans were detailed and definitive. He wanted each child to come off the court having understood the benefits of why a particular adjustment had been made to one or more of their grips, strokes or movements. His eagle eye was always fixed on each. Barkers' way was not to be totally authoritarian, rather to be firm, and importantly too, have a fun experience in the learning environment. Feeding tennis balls as if his pupils were part of a production line wouldn't cut it. Neither would standing by a net post observing match play drills. Interaction with every pupil on court, manoeuvring them into correct positions and teaching them about the geometry of the tennis court and where to hit the ball, couldn't possibly be done by the coach standing to one side."

Patrick (Pat) Cash

Not long after his Avvenire Cup success, Pat Cash made the quarter-finals of the French Open Boys' Singles where he lost to Mats Wilander. He then took to the grass courts of England for the first time. Having not long turned 16, he played well enough to reach the final of the Wimbledon Boys' Singles where he lost to American Matt Anger. At times he used the serve and volley tactic that Barclay urged him to employ.

On Cash's return home from Europe, at the age of just 16 years, he won the Victorian Hardcourt Men's Singles title, held at Grace Park.

The coach took a step back, looked at the big picture and the powerful athlete he had before him in Pat Cash. He had put in an incredible performance with Mark Hartnett in Europe on the clay in 1980 and then again the following year. If he was to be a future contender for some of the biggest singles tournaments around the world, particularly those held on grass, he would need to add a serve and volley game to his repertoire. Cash's game from the baseline had always been very sound. Barclay was often asked whether Cash served and volleyed during his early overseas trips. "No, generally the only time he went to the net was to shake hands," he joked. Cash remembered being called a bit of a hacker. "I was a base liner, but was taught to volley early on by Barkers and was often encouraged to venture up to the net." Barclay's updated plan was to go all out to develop Cash's serve and volley game. The coach upped the ante. This led to increased hours spent drilling Cash both on his volley and smash, the latter having had been a particularly weak shot. Being a perfectionist, in combination with at times a volatile personality, missed smashes by Cash often resulted in smashed racquets spread across the practice court.

The muscular Cash would pester Barclay during his on-court sessions. "Just one more hit, Barkers," the young tyro would plead, even when the coach was packing up to go to the house for dinner. It could easily be late into the evening and Barclay would still be on the court further tweaking Cash's game. Neither wanted to finish a session until they had corrected whatever was needed. That was the inner drive, determination and belief playing itself out between the two. That was Barclay and Cash going to the nth degree.

Barclay continued to work on Cash's game through the back half of the year. Another of the coach's friends in Melbourne, Chris Gleeson, was involved in selling medical equipment. He helped finance Barclay and Cash's next independent overseas tennis trip to North America. This took in the Canadian Boys' Singles, which Cash won, and the US Open Boys' Singles where he reached the semi-final. Pat Cash followed up his good results in North America by making the final of the Australian Open Junior Boys' Singles at the end of the year and put himself in line to be the world's top-ranked junior. A straight-sets loss in the final to Swede Jorgen Windahl put that opportunity on hold.

Barclay's juniors continued to feature on the world stage. In the same 1981 year, Cash had his first foray into the Australian Open Men's Singles where he lost to former titleholder, Mark Edmondson. Sharon Hodgkin won the Australian Open Girls' Doubles with Tasmanian Maree Booth.

Barclay's stocks grew as 1982 proved yet another big leap in Pat Cash's career. He defeated Swede Henrik Sundstrom 6-4, 6-7, 6-3 to win the Wimbledon Boys' Singles final and then Frenchman Guy Forget 6-3, 6-3 in the US Boys' Singles final a few months later. He partnered his previous year's MATCH team mate John Frawley to reach the Boys' Doubles final.

Bernadette Randall, together with American Anne Hulbert, also reached the Girls' Doubles final at the same tournament.

Barclay paid particular tribute to some of the senior players on tour. "All the older Aussie players were a wonderful help to Pat. Kim Warwick helped him out at the US Juniors. Kim worked his butt off every morning for us and the kids didn't start until the second week of the event. Kim himself went on to defeat French great Yannick Noah in the fourth round of the Men's Singles and reached the quarter-finals, so it worked both ways."

The significance of Pat Cash's potential, performance and results was poignant. Barclay then saw his number one charge get a call-up for Australia's Davis Cup duties, selected as the traditional orange boy and hitting partner for the team on the eve of its October semi-final clash against the United States, to be held in Perth. Australian team member John Fitzgerald, who played in the quarter-final clash against Chile, had already come across Barclay in 1979. Aged 19, while competing at the Australian Open at Kooyong, he had walked down between the rows of the outside grass courts and noticed young Cash playing a junior match. He spoke to an observing Barclay about the young prospect, clearly impressed by both player and coach.

Late into the year, Cash won the Australian Men's Hardcourt Singles title, defeating Sydney's Craig Miller. Already possessing a solid serve, with Barclay's guidance, he developed a big kick serve, which he used to get the ball high up onto his right-handed opponent's backhand side, thus creating opportunities to get to the net and finish points. Mark Hartnett was back playing and at the end of the year he won the Australian Open Boys' Doubles title with Melbourne player Brendan Burke.

Barclay now believed Pat Cash was ready to step up onto the big stage. The end of 1982 saw the 17-year-old reach the quarter-finals of the Australian Open Men's Singles where he was defeated by fellow Aussie Paul McNamee. The result gave Barclay great heart.

Cash made the semi-final of the Men's Volvo Grand Prix South Australian Singles, then competed in the Victorian Open, held at Kooyong. Having successfully worked his way through the draw, he had to contend with the massive serve of giant American Mike Gandolfo in the quarter-final. Barclay instructed Cash to do whatever he could to get the return of serve back into play and force his opponent to play shots, as he believed Gandolfo's serve was a long way ahead of the rest of his game. The young Victorian followed his coach's advice to the letter, to then make his way through the semis and on to reach the final. There he defeated former 1981 Wimbledon Singles semi-finalist and fellow Australian Rod Frawley 6-4, 7-6 in the final. Said Barclay, "Pat served with great consistency, returned well and hit his first volley unbelievably well." In addition to his best serve, that being into his opponent's body, Barclay believed that because Pat served and followed through into the court with his back foot first, it also allowed him to swing his serve very wide to Frawley's forehand side, at times making the shot unreturnable. When Frawley changed his returning position to cover that serve, it opened up the centre for a tactical change in direction. It also caused him to wear out the dimples in many of his right-foot shoes. Similarly, it was a serving movement Barclay adopted early in his own tennis, which proved especially effective on grass courts.

At the time, Patrick Cash was the youngest player to win a professional tour title.

Winning the Victorian Open title lifted his world ranking from 342 to 44. On accepting prize money, he turned professional. Barclay thought a top ten world singles ranking was achievable. Although proud of this first triumph at the professional level, Barclay was in no doubt that the bigger challenges would come from yet again playing abroad, this time against the men, on all surfaces.

Backyard Tennis Court

Another move was afoot for the Barclay family. In 1982, they shifted to nearby Park Orchards, a suburb littered with large blocks of land. There was enough room to build a tennis court in the coach's backyard. Both Dean and Brad moved from Mitcham High School to the inner city St Kevin's Boys' Catholic College to further their secondary school education. Sister Toni-Ann moved to Yarra Valley Grammar School in Ringwood.

Ian's precious home court in Park Orchards

Soon enough, in early 1983, the construction of the new home tennis court commenced. As a mark of his loyalty, Barclay offered the job to fellow Heatherdale Tennis Club member, Peter Bland, a surveyor and handyman, who was only too keen to lend a hand. Other club members lent both manpower and machinery for the job.

Once the excavation and drainage were complete, wheelbarrow loads of scoria were carefully eased down a steep descent on one side of the house to the site.

At one point, a fully laden trailer slipped from its handler's grasp and started rolling down a steep descent. Fortunately, it turned sideways on itself, preventing a potential disaster. The job also entailed erecting a high retainer wall one side of the court using wooden garden sleepers.

Hot weather accompanied the building of the court. Barclay and his crew frequently took quick dips in the family's swimming pool to cool off, before trudging back up the block for the next wheelbarrow load. At the time, Victoria was experiencing a spate of bushfires, several of which had already destroyed many lives and homes. Most notably one of Victoria's most infamous days, Ash Wednesday fell on a day while the coach and his crew were working. With fires raging around the outskirts of Melbourne and the temperature in some areas reaching 43 degrees, several small spot fires began to flare up across the road in an adjacent nature reserve as a result of the roaming embers. Before long, tennis court labourers became firefighters, blanketing out small spot fires less than 100 metres away from the house.

The court was laid with the traditional en tout cas surface. However, Barclay decided he would mix in a very fine blend of crushed brick, which was more powderlike in texture. He wanted the tennis ball to bounce similar to that of the clay courts he had encountered in Europe two years earlier. Once the surface was laid, he spent hours, day after day and week after week spreading new topping. At the same time, he rolled, swept and watered his new court until it settled to his satisfaction. Importantly for Barclay, one more tennis court built meant more players could hit more tennis balls more often. An additional bonus was that now his club Heatherdale had lighting on six of its eight courts.

Barclay spent hour after hour, day after day fine-tuning Cash's game on the new home court in Park Orchards. "Pat spent so many hours training at our house, we thought at times we had another brother," said daughter Toni-Ann. Basket after basket of tennis balls were hit come rain, hail or shine, sometimes late into the night, aimed at better developing his all-round game. Mark Hartnett was back in Melbourne and acted as a hitting partner for his mate Cash.

From age 13, young Echuca country junior Andrew Crossman resided at the Barclay house on a part-time basis while still making the weekly journey down from Echuca. Said Crossman, "Many young players from all over the world came to be taught by Barkers on the backyard court and to further their tennis. Some would stay for a period of time and become a part of the Barclay family.

"If Jackie cooked for one, at any time she could easily be cooking for 21. The kids ate and slept tennis and went away from their home better players and people for the experience. If Barkers wasn't feeding balls to Pat, Mark, Bernadette or me, he was up on the roof clearing gutters, or wheelbarrowing more topping for his tennis court or doing anything required around the yard. He was a workaholic." Crossman too joined the Wednesday afternoon squad.

When at home in Australia, whether in Park Orchards or at Heatherdale, Barclay still ran his private lessons, coaching classes and squads. Said Will Coghlan, "It didn't matter who stepped onto the tennis court. Over time, Ian still got just as much satisfaction working with his elite juniors as he did seeing half a dozen brand new baby beginners run onto the tennis court for the first time, with a huge smile on their face, and then run off again with the same smile."

The effect that Barclay's guidance had on his assistant coaches was immeasurable. As Ann Quinn completed her Human Movement Degree and Diploma of Education, she hungered to learn more. Each time Barclay came back from an overseas trip, she would absorb any new ideas and knowledge that he had picked up from his travels. Barclay's mind was always looking ahead. As an example, he had seen the grip for the forehand drive move away from the eastern forehand towards a semi-western grip, which could help create more topspin. He knew this evolutionary element of the game would only help his Australian juniors if they were to catch up with the rest of the world. This notion stood in the face of tradition, because, for example, the Australian Open was still being played on grass and the national coaching course for prospective professional coaches didn't subscribe to his grip theory. However, Barclay felt he needed to challenge the norm.

Quinn believed he was way ahead of his time compared to other coaches in the sport. Quinn and Barclay's other assistants also felt challenged and it set the tone for trying to find new ways to advance his students. This was a great carrot for young Pat Cash as he was a perfectionist himself and was prepared to go to every length in order to improve his game and find an edge. Video analysis, already a major component of Barclay's coaching, became even more prominent.

Several keenly wanted to further themselves within the profession. In her last year of university, Ann Quinn wrote some 300 letters looking for work overseas. Her mission was to spend a further year developing her knowledge through studying what the best coaches in various other sports were doing with their athletes in foreign countries. Quinn received 72 job offers. She took a working holiday to America and had a lot of opportunities to coach elite juniors and throughout Europe. She also landed the prestigious job as Health and Fitness Director at the Nick Bollittierri Tennis Academy in Florida. Her one year overseas turned into five years and she regularly remained in close touch with Barclay.

On Friday nights during the winter at the end of the coaching week at Heatherdale, it was standard practice to have a drink at the Manhattan Hotel for both Barclay and his assistants. The week's coaching was discussed and with it more knowledge gained about the game. So too was discussion had about the upcoming round of VFL matches. The next day, some of the tennis club's avid football followers would then bundle into the coach's car for the trip out to Waverley Park football ground to watch his beloved Hawthorn's weekend match.

Some of Barclay's top Heatherdale students from his Wednesday squad, including Mark Hartnett, Rohan Goetzke, Lisa Keller, Daniel Carroll and Wes Horskins continued playing tennis at a high level. Through one of Barclay's many contacts,

Hartnett gained an airfare and accommodation to travel to Switzerland and play club tennis for the Dalholzie Tennis Club, near the capital Bern. He stayed for six years, played tournaments on the professional tour and also coached.

Goetzke undertook an Engineering Degree at Swinburne University in Hawthorn before heading to Europe to play at different levels on the professional circuit. He then settled in Belgium.

Keller who had consistently held top state junior rankings, often representing Victoria in teams' events, played Division One NCAA College in America, club tennis in Germany and Switzerland and competed at the Australian Open.

Horskins gained a scholarship to Oklahoma State University, then played on the pro tour for several years, once making the main draw at the Australian Open. He lived and played in Fuengirola, Spain for three years, where he too also coached. Carroll too went overseas to play on the tour.

Davis Cup

Not long into 1983, Pat Cash was summoned by Australian Davis Cup captain and tennis legend, Neale for his major representative debut.

From his own early junior days under Brian Slattery's coaching, Fraser went on to have an outstanding tennis career. He won a total of 19 Grand Slam titles, including the 1960 Wimbledon and 1959 and 1960 US Open Men's Singles. He had also captained Australia to its 1973 and 1977 Davis Cup wins.

Barclay's initial thought was that it was a pretty tough call on his young player, as he was still just a kid, at 17 years and nine months. On the other side of the coin, Barclay also believed it was the greatest honour to represent one's country. From his early coaching days, he told every student that playing Davis Cup and Federation Cup (female equivalent) should always be their number one goal.

Up until this time in Davis Cup tennis, private coaches had little if no involvement in matches, simply because the captain ran most of the proceedings. Neale Fraser's methods ran accordingly, but gradually changed. Knowing that Cash at times had problems with both his game and volatile temperament, Fraser felt he might need to turn to Barclay for some advice. Barclay knew that on the one hand, if anyone tried to put the fire out in Pat, he would struggle to play his best tennis, but at the same time, he himself could be the calming influence on the team's newest member.

To have Barclay on hand was invaluable for other reasons too. He was on the road a lot, knew most of the players on the tour, their strengths and their weaknesses. He also spent plenty of time around practice courts. He would pick up valuable pointers on opposing players' habits, temperaments and even important little things like ball toss placements, which would determine the type of serve a player was going to hit. This was vital information that he could pass on to Fraser.

Australia's first Davis Cup tie was played against Great Britain on grass at Memorial Drive in Adelaide in early March. Cash felt the pressure of expectation and his pre-match anxiety during practice resulted in him breaking every racquet in his bag. Unable to quickly get more racquets and to the required specifications, Barclay hurriedly had some sent from Slazenger, although 35 gms heavier than usual. The coach then had to bevel down the edges of each in order to make them lighter.

Barclay took his seat alongside the other squad members in the front row. After a first day washout, Cash defeated 1977 Australian Open finalist John Lloyd 8-6 in a marathon fifth set of the opening rubber. Barclay felt the incredibly hard-fought tennis the young teenager played against Lloyd helped set the tie up for the Australians.

A win against Great Britain was followed by a 5-0 quarter-final victory against Romania in Brisbane during July and a 4-1 semi-final win against France in Sydney at the end of September. That took Australia into a home final against Sweden, to be staged at the end of December, yet again on the grass, this time at the home of tennis in Melbourne, Kooyong.

In the meantime, between Davis Cup victories, Cash secured his second Volvo Grand Prix professional tour singles title at the GWA Mazda Classic in Brisbane in early October, played on carpet. He defeated fellow Australian Paul McNamee in the final in three sets, 4-6, 6-4, 6-3.

Two of Barclay's MATCH girls also tasted great success. Ex-student Elizabeth Minter won the US Girls' Singles, defeating American Marianne Werdel 6-3, 7-5. Like her older sister Anne, she had also been a national junior titleholder and won numerous tournaments in her home country, before too ultimately progressing on to the main WTA professional tour. In going forward with her own career, she played Federation Cup, was a singles finalist on the tour in Zagreb in 1995 and won two doubles titles, one with sister Anne. Elizabeth attained a career-high singles ranking of 66 in 1987.

Bernadette Randall won the US Open Girls' Doubles final, again partnering Anne Hulbert to defeat Russian players Natasha Reva and Larisa Savchenko 6-4, 6-2, with Barclay courtside for the match. At one point he became somewhat nervous, as his eye caught sight of several security figures hovering close by. Only days before, the Russian military had shot down a Korean passenger airliner that had flown into Russian airspace, killing all 269 passengers and crew members. The incident had dramatically increased tensions between the world's two super powers.

In December, Randall won the Australian Open Girls' Doubles with New South Wales girl Kim Staunton and was runner-up in the Girls' Singles. Randall's great performances brought with it significant reward. Through the year, she attained the number one doubles and number two world junior singles ranking. Running parallel to and then post her junior career, Randall also competed on the WTA tour as well as in Grand Slam events. She recorded a number of good wins, particularly on grass, at both the Australian Open and Wimbledon before ultimately falling to a career-ending elbow injury.

Things soured somewhat before the Davis Cup final had even begun. To Barclay, the source wasn't a complete surprise. John Newcombe's newspaper column leading into the Davis Cup final stated that comparing Swedish number one player Mats Wilander with Cash was like comparing "the Grand Canyon with a crack in the wall" (Pat Cash – *Uncovered*).

The article was very hurtful to Barclay, Cash and both families. It further fuelled their scepticism and dislike of the media, but if anything, only served to spur them on.

Newcombe had a number of unsavoury articles written about the coach and his young player over the years. Other journalists had been much fairer, often steering away from fabricated, made-up controversial stories about the two. "The tall poppy syndrome in Australia was clearly evident," remarked Barclay. "In America, if you made it, or did anything of note, you would be put on a pedestal and revered. You would stay there and very few people would say nasty things about you. Here, it doesn't matter what you've done for your country, there will come a time when the media just cuts your feet from underneath you. We have followed in the footsteps of the British press and their tabloids."

Toni-Ann Barclay was adamant that her father's detractors only served to fuel the competitive edge within the family. "Those who said Dad would never make a player out of Pat just drove him and the family to compete harder and stronger. It gave us a smug feeling whenever Pat won something of note."

Australia's opponent in the final was Sweden, whose team consisted of Mats Wilander, Joakim Nystrom, Anders Jarryd and Hans Simmonson. The home team included Cash, John Fitzgerald, Paul McNamee and Mark Edmondson.

Cash believed he was up to the challenge but couldn't account for the recently crowned Australian Open winner Wilander in the opening singles rubber, losing 3-6, 6-4, 7-9, 3-6. However, Fitzgerald superbly squared the tie against the second string Nystrom, 6-4, 6-2, 4-6, 6-4. The doubles went the way of the Aussies, which gave them the opportunity to wrap up the tie in the fourth rubber.

Barclay was wary of how steady a player Nystrom was and equally aware of the pressure on his young tyro's shoulders for the all-important reverse singles. He also knew that if Cash played to his best level he could win.

Although coming off a sleepless night and suffering predictable pre-match nerves, Cash the baby of the team, wearing his signature black and white chequered headband, capitalised on the fast court. Using an accurate serve and brilliant net game, he steamrolled past his opponent 6-4, 6-1, 6-1 to seal the Davis Cup win for his country and in the process become the youngest player, at 18 years and 7 months, to win a deciding rubber of a Davis Cup match. Barclay felt great pride in the team's victory and his player, so young in Davis Cup terms, to be able to lead the way and handle a situation way beyond expectations.

Barclay gradually became an unofficial member of the Davis Cup team.

Widely recognised as a tough, uncompromising, international competition, those who had represented their country in Davis Cup knew what pressures teams had to endure in order to obtain the ultimate prize.

Barclay felt the result at least quietened a few of their doubters.

During Davis Cup ties, then Australian Prime Minister Bob Hawke, a tennis fan, often rang Barclay to check on Cash's progress.

During conversations about tennis, he would also pass on odd tips to Barclay for Sydney race meetings.

The coach admired the working man, Rhode Scholar and fellow punter in Hawke.

Bob Hawke, who became a friend of Ian's, pictured sitting in the front row watching Cash during the 1983 Davis Cup final

John Fitzgerald appreciated his presence at Davis Cup time. "Barkers played a very significant role in our Davis Cup campaigns. Cashy was Australia's gun player, but could be prone to periods of volatility. Barkers could handle that side of him well, particularly just prior to Cup ties when practice was intense and team selection was nigh. When nerves and tension grew around the squad, Barkers provided a steadying influence to all of the players."

Out on the professional tour, Fitzgerald spent many hours around Barclay as the Australian players invariably practised together before tournaments.

"Barkers was unashamedly supportive of Pat on tour, but he was also supportive of Pat's contemporaries and a friend to many. He was only too willing to offer advice if called upon," Fitzgerald added, and drew comparisons with his native South Australian coach, Peter Smith. "If I had grown up playing tennis in Victoria, Barkers is definitely the coach I would have been drawn to. As the son of a farmer, I question whether I could have afforded him, but his dedication, knowledge and time given to his kids definitely would have attracted me."

At the US Open during the early 1980s, Fitzgerald shared the same practice court as Barclay. Somehow the coach found himself in the firing line of a Fitzgerald smash when not looking and got hit in the throat. The force of the shot put him on the floor. Fitzgerald quickly ran towards the prostrate coach, feeling distraught at what had just occurred. "Barkers couldn't speak for five or ten minutes afterwards, which was a rare thing for him," quipped Fitzgerald. "To this day he still jokingly reminds me that I nearly finished off his coaching career."

The middle of 1984 saw Cash reach his first Grand Slam Men's Singles semi-final at Wimbledon.

Facing the number-one-ranked player, the brilliant but feisty American left-hander, John McEnroe, Barclay warned him not to allow McEnroe to get the mental edge over him. At the drop of a hat, McEnroe could start an argument with an umpire or yell out to someone in the crowd with the clear intent of distracting his opponent.

Adhering to his coach's words, Cash played with broad shoulders and chest out, ironically at one stage nearly knocking McEnroe to the ground at the change of ends. This was not enough however as he lost to the American in straight sets.

Ian with star pupil, Pat Cash

The Canadian Open, held in Toronto was next in early August. Cash played American Jimmy Connors in the third round. Barclay and Cash had watched Connors several times on the practice court. They had taken note of his high level of intensity, which always reflected in his match play.

They realised how hard he had worked to get to the top. Barclay suggested that if he could defeat Connors, he could drive back home in a limousine, just like the sort Connors had arrived in. The coach told his young charge not to lose concentration with what Connors got up to during the match, as he had already had two line officials sent off the court up to that date. Losing to Connors in straight sets, the limousine ride would have to wait.

At the US Open three months later, Cash reached another semi-final, this time against world number two, Ivan Lendl. Barclay remembered the tournament for several reasons. Cash was running out of racquets. He had smashed plenty up to that point. Barclay's role was extended again. More racquets were ordered and quickly airfreighted in. They were to be collected from a depot, located several miles from the main J F Kennedy airport terminal in the dingy borough of Queens.

Cautious, Barclay caught a taxi, which dropped him off a number of blocks away, with the driver declaring it wasn't a very safe part of town. This was cold comfort to Barclay. He didn't know the area and the thought of who or what may lie between him and Cash's box of new tennis racquets sent a shiver through him. Houses were boarded up, cars had been stripped, with some up on blocks, and engines stolen. He looked over his shoulder every step of the way until eventually he located the front gates to the depot. Once inside the door, Barclay joined a small line of people similarly collecting items. Standing close to the front of the line, he noticed some huge, angry-looking male black truck drivers. One bypassed the queue and sauntered up to the front desk. "This guy could have been an American football linebacker, he was that big," recalled Barclay. "The big man slammed his paperwork on the desk, turned to those in the line and said, "Any of you here got a problem with me?" Too scared, no one replied."

No sooner had he got the carton of racquets, then Barclay was out the door. With his white hair shining in the glow of the dimmed streetlights, he took one of the racquets from the box and held it tightly to protect himself if needed. He took off and moved swiftly through the small dark streets, until he found his way back to the motel room.

He declared to room mate Martin Kozma he had never been so scared in all his life and decided the next trip he would take would be in the morning, to the nearest clothes store for some new underwear.

Barclay sat next to legendary American player and former world number one Pancho Segura in the coaches' box for the semi-final. Segura liked the Aussies and rooted heavily for Cash. Playing attacking tennis, Cash held two match points against Lendl deep in the fifth set. Lendl hit a remarkable mishit defensive lob over his head off a superb down-the-line volley, which landed on the baseline. He then agonisingly saw a service ace, hit down the centreline wrongly called out.

American female legend, Billie Jean King, who had been commentating the match, called Barclay into the studio afterwards. She showed him the replay of the crucial serve, which with heavy kick had been called out a split second before landing. Heartbreak twice for coach and student as the Czech prevailed in five sets. Such was the standard of tennis played, Barclay thought Cash might have been a reasonable chance to beat McEnroe in the final had he got through.

The Playing Coach

Ian Barclay's life took a forced change of direction midway through 1985. Pat Cash's legs had been giving him trouble through the early part of the year. A combination of hard training, which included time spent with their beloved Hawthorn Football Club, hitting hundreds of tennis balls and developing a changed playing style, which demanded so much of his body, all came to a head.

At Davis Cup team mate Paul McNamee's base, situated at Harry Hopman's tennis camp in Largo, Florida, Cash twinged his back during a nondescript warm-up stretch before a practice hit. It got worse across the next few tournaments. At one stage during a practice session on the eve of Wimbledon's lead-up event at the Queen's Club, the Stella Artois tournament, he put his back out. Barclay had to get him into the back seat of a car, raise his feet and get him to a local osteopath. Invariably playing in pain, Cash crawled his way through to Wimbledon, where his last match for the year would be in the doubles final with John Fitzgerald.

In reality, Barclay's gun player had succumbed to a serious, major back injury. After undergoing a CAT scan back at Melbourne's Epworth Hospital, the seriousness of Cash's injury was confirmed, as herniated discs L4 and L5 in his lower back. He opted not to have traditional back surgery, in preference for a relatively new but potentially high-risk procedure. It involved an injection of chymopapain, a drug which contained extracts from the paw paw fruit. The treatment was followed by a substantial lay off, for the next eight months.

Barclay realised he needed to stay active as well as keep some income coming in. He decided while those in the medical and sports science fields looked after Cash, he would spend time competing himself. He took to the Seniors Tour and played in the Dubler Cup teams' event, the equivalent of the Davis Cup for the Over 45 age group, played in Perth.

Although the temperatures reached over 40 degrees, Barclay's form and fitness was good, due mainly to the hard work he had done with Cash. The Australian team made the final. Although admitting to some severe nerves, Barclay held on to win his singles in three sets, albeit the Australian team being defeated by Germany.

In action at the 1985 International Over 45s at Kooyong

A week later, the Phillip Morris International veterans' tennis championships 45 Years and Over title was played in Melbourne, at Kooyong. Barclay was seeded eighth. 128 entrants made up a strong main draw.

With the teams' event having just been held in Perth, many of the overseas players stayed on and went to Melbourne.

Barclay suspected that no one gave him a chance to win the tournament. Light in stature, he only weighed around 10 stone. At 47 years, he had been injury free for many years and was still nimble around the court.

Barclay comfortably made his way through the draw. His first serve and volley percentage remained high throughout the tournament. Where he could, as often as possible, he would try and play his preferred tactic, that of playing the ball behind his opposition in order to get to the net for the easy put-away volley or smash.

After each match he rang Cash, McNamee and Peter McNamara in the US to let them know how he was progressing. Every time the coach rang, they rattled and banged pots and pans together in applause, which nearly deafened Barclay on the other end of the phone.

He won his quarter-final 7-5 in the third set and the semi-final by the same score. Leading 6-2, 4-1, 0-40 in the final on centre court, Barclay had been well on top of his German opponent, Klaus Fuhrmann. "At that stage the guy did his block and I thought I had him then," said Barclay. "All of a sudden he hit four unreturnable serves and then blew me off the court for eight games straight. Although I felt tight as the match went on, fortunately deep in the third set he choked more and I ran out the tiebreaker to take the title."

Barclay had played 13 singles and doubles matches in seven days, again in fierce heat, the temperature passing 40 degrees daily. He believed the win helped silence a few of his critics, who'd questioned his on-court playing ability and therefore his credentials to coach a player to the highest level of tennis. The win also led to Barclay being offered some invitations into several other seniors' tournaments around the world.

Barclay embraced the opportunity and headed to Newport Beach, California soon after. He won the Over 45 Singles final again, then had the memorable experience of being paired up in the combined 110 years doubles with the infamous American tennis hustler, 67-year-old Bobby Riggs. Riggs had won three Grand Slam Singles titles during his career towards the end of the 1930s. He was arguably better remembered for his famous Battle of the Sexes challenges later during the 1970s against the world's best women players. He first challenged Australian female legend Margaret Court in Ramona, California in what became known as the "Mother's Day Massacre" in May of 1973, defeating her in straight sets 6-2, 6-1. He then played American great Billie Jean King later in the same year at the Houston Astrodome in Texas for a $100,000 winner-take-all prize, and lost 6-4, 6-3, 6-3.

Seeing Riggs for the first time, Barclay said, "He looked like he'd had that many face lifts, his belly button had worked its way up to become the dimple on his chin. His hair was dyed a carrot red colour and he looked an absolute spiv of the first kind. Not only that, his tennis bag was full of all the dirty tricks one could imagine." Riggs' much younger wife told Barclay that if any of their opponents wised up to some of her husband's antics during their matches, an escape via the closest exit door might be his best strategy.

Barclay and Riggs won the doubles event. Riggs pestered Barclay to stop coaching Cash and join him on his own tennis journey, where he promised to make the coach a wealthy man.

One night, Riggs called Barclay to his hotel room. He told his younger partner he could make him $1000 richer downstairs by the bar quicker than the coach could blink and that Barclay had to be his straight man. One of Riggs' favourite tricks was to produce a brand-new deck of playing cards, place a rubbish bin about two metres away, then flick the cards into the bin, one at a time. He would catch the eye of a big noter who would fall for his trick. With all the players showered up after the day's play, many were in the bar having a drink. Riggs commenced throwing cards into the bin, at the same time raising his voice, challenging the crowd to bet against him landing all 52 cards into the bin in a row.

Sure enough, a small crowd had gathered and one man stepped forward and bet $20 against him. After 30 cards Riggs missed, the punter made his collect and Barclay the banker handed over the cash.

The next punter came up and bet $50. This time he got to the 40th card and missed again. Barclay paid out again. This went on a bit longer.

A moustached man wearing a Stetson confidently stepped forward and duly laid a $1000 bet. Riggs whispered across to his banker, "Here comes your $1000." He then proceeded to flick the entire pack into the bin, without flinching. Barclay was stunned. Riggs' wife later remarked that she thought they could never lose on the court because of Barclay's fitness, and neither in the bar with her husband's hustling, but it was probably fortunate he was leaving the next day.

Barclay was amazed that for a man his age, Riggs' finger dexterity was as good with his tennis as it was with his cards. "He could hit the ball onto lines and within inches of his targets with monotonous regularity. I had a great time with Bobby. He had a great mind for the game of tennis, as well as for the hustle." Other American tennis greats Pancho Gonzales and Gardner Molloy were a part of the same circuit. Barclay found it amusing that like Riggs, many players were accompanied by wives half their age.

Back Home

Back at home in Park Orchards later that year, Barclay received a telephone call. It was from a woman in the small remote south-west Victorian farming township of Balmoral, situated about 300 kilometres to the west of Melbourne. On making the call, she cited the lack of opportunity for the children in her town and the wider region to access any professional tennis coaching. She told him she had opened the telephone book and looked under 'TENNIS COACHES'. Starting at the top alphabetically, but without any success to date, she had worked her way down the list and found his name.

Her pleasant manner, enthusiasm and plea for help won him over. Once again, with the car loaded with tennis balls, racquets, tennis ball machine and assistant coaches, it was off to another country town, this time for a five-day clinic. The country setting was a nice change from the daily grind of the city, as was the local hospitality. "The kids at Balmoral were just so keen to learn, impress and improve their tennis every day. The courts were hard and hot in the fierce December summer weather. The colour of the balls changed from yellow to black very quickly on the bitumen surface. But the kids didn't care. If they fell over, they would get straight back up and just go again," said Barclay. The clinic became his annual event.

Such was Barclay's growing demand in the game back in Melbourne, prior to one Balmoral clinic, he had inadvertently booked a sportsman's speaking engagement for 7.30 pm back in the city, coinciding with the final day of the clinic. In attempting to meet his deadline, he ran out the gate once the final ball had been hit, said goodbye to the kids then swapped his tennis gear for a dinner suit and started the three-and-a-half-hour drive back to Melbourne.

The road out of town was mostly sealed, but long and narrow. Considering the isolated location and the seemingly quiet road ahead, Barclay decided to push down hard on the accelerator. Suddenly, on reaching the peak of a small incline, he came face to face with an old Holden utility stacked high with hay bales. Barclay was flying and almost airborne as both vehicles veered quickly onto each side of the road. Each flicked up gravel, stones and dust, but somehow managed to stay in control as they passed each other by.

Rocky Loccisano, another student who had recently transitioned to the role of assistant coach, was back at the local Balmoral hotel with the remaining coaches celebrating the clinic's end. The driver of the utility burst through the door of the hotel and yelled out, "Some fucking idiot in a blue sports car just flew past me back down the road and I swear he was flying as high as my bales of hay." Loccisano replied, "That was Barkers." To which the farmer replied, "Yeah, and the bloke was wearing a dinner suit. If I ever see him again, I'll kill him."

Over 30 years later and the same clinic is still conducted by ex-student, Andrew Crossman.

Returning Overseas

As Pat Cash rehabilitated, Barclay rejoined the team. Late into the year, Cash tested his back out by playing some doubles in Palm Springs. Barclay spent most of his time fending off questions from the media about Cash's new Norwegian girlfriend Anne-Britt and her pregnancy to him.

Meanwhile, whilst Ann Quinn was completing her Master's Degree in Biomechanics and Exercise Physiology and finishing her thesis on abdominal and lower back muscle involvement in tennis, she received a call from Cash. With his back injury well documented, he was keen to catch up with Quinn hopeful she may be of assistance in his quest to return to the men's professional tour. He wanted to rebuild his fitness to a level that hopefully would prevent the injury from recurring.

Quinn had used Cash years earlier as a subject for various physical tests and assignments, while studying her Human Movement Degree, so knew the athlete well. She thought the chance to work again with him would be a wonderful opportunity not only to help Cash but also to repay Barclay for the opportunities he had given her in pursuit of her own career. Thinking she may spend a couple of months helping out, little did she realise it would be a major part of her life for the next 10 years.

Not long after becoming a father for the first time to son Daniel Patrick, Cash flew back to the US to begin training with Quinn and prepare for his comeback at Wimbledon. Said Quinn, "We had to start from scratch as he had very little base and build his strength, power and endurance." She remained in the US to complete the final few weeks of her Master's Degree and Cash headed to London.

Rocky Loccisano was trying his hand playing on the overseas satellite circuit. To help out his coach, he went to London and acted as a hitting partner for Cash, Then out of the blue, Cash suffered an appendicitis attack and needed urgent surgery.

Quinn cancelled her trip to London, thinking he would not be ready to play at The All England Club, where he had been granted a wild card. However, the determined young player was not prepared to give up the great Wimbledon opportunity. Instructions were given to the surgeon not to cut any muscles so he could heal quickly and Cash was on the phone to Quinn daily, getting specific exercises to do from his hospital bed. Within a day of the operation, he was on the hospital bike and doing gentle exercises.

Three days later, he was back on court doing some gentle hitting. Seventeen days later, he rewrote the medical books and was playing at Wimbledon. He reached the Men's Singles quarter-finals where he lost to Frenchman Henri Leconte in four sets. Quinn believed his extraordinary condition and determination was the only reason he had recovered so quickly in time from his operation.

Now that her Master's Degree was finished, Quinn spent the next six months training Cash full time and travelling with him throughout the US. She oversaw his entire fitness regime. Two of the major conditioning areas she worked on with Cash were in his agility and movement. She changed his diet, worked on his recovery and made sure he was energised. Cash devoted himself to the programs she devised. While working with Cash she often sought out Barclay for additional advice.

Barclay knew his star pupil was in good hands. Player and trainer often worked out on a distant back court at tournaments. Cash could be seen running to all directions of the court, at times using a variety of unusual looking exercise equipment such as medicine balls, resistance bands and lots of speed equipment, which these days is standard practice. Although they generally sought the sanctum of privacy, Cash and Quinn often attracted a crowd.

Quinn often sat alongside Barclay during Cash's matches. Barclay and Cash knew each other inside out and back to front in relation to the young man's game. He would lean across and whisper to her where Cash was going to serve on an upcoming big point or what tactic he was about to employ. She would often laugh in amazement and ask Barclay whether he had some sort of earpiece connected to his player, as Cash would always do exactly what his coach wanted him to do.

Such had become the demands on her time and Quinn's clientele extended to include Australian Test cricketers Merv Hughes and Simon O'Donnell (who had battled cancer), VFL club Essendon (where she had worked as a fitness advisor) and four-time Women's Grand Slam Singles winner Hana Mandlikova

Full-time Touring Coach

Heatherdale Tennis Club realised with the amount of time Barclay was spending overseas, something had to give. He had been the professional tennis coach at the club for 13 years. He had spoilt the club with his dedication, enthusiasm, professionalism and undeniable passion for its development over a long period. The club had grown into arguably the strongest and most successful local tennis club in metropolitan Melbourne through the 1970s and 1980s, regularly producing outstanding junior talent.

Under Barclay it could claim the bragging rights to having been the developing ground for multiple state, national and international junior singles and doubles champions (including Grand Slam junior titleholders), players who had represented their state and country in national and international junior teams and senior Davis Cup and Federation Cup teams, as well as players who had moved onto the tough, uncompromising professional circuit. Sixteen senior club championship singles titles had been won by his pupils.

Of equal importance was the introduction that Barclay had given to hundreds of new children of all ages to the game of tennis. The efforts of others around him had been enormous. Along with wife Jackie's pivotal role, the volunteers at the Heatherdale Tennis Club who ran the club organised the competitions and created many other opportunities for all his juniors, had helped his cause no end and were owed an enormous debt of gratitude.

Both parties reached a mutual decision that Barclay take on a role of Director of Coaching at the club, in order that he could still oversee the entire coaching program and have an involvement at the club when back in Australia.

The head coaching role was handed down to yet another in the line of his assistant coaches, Mike Spruzen.

Barclay continued to build the team around Pat Cash. With Ann Quinn now well entrenched as fitness advisor and David Zuker his physiotherapist, the Australian Institute of Sport psychologist Jeff Bond was added to the team, the appointment organised by Quinn. Cash had only ever regarded psychologists as good for basket cases, having scant regard for the industry. On his father's long-standing concerns about his son, Cash accepted some help. Quinn also convinced him of the importance of the mental game too, having incorporated relaxation, visualisation and a lot of positive psychology work into her on-court workouts.

Of the growing entourage, Barclay confided in Quinn and Bond the most. "Ann's job was to make Cash as fit and fast as hands could make him and Jeff's was to get his mind on the job the whole time."

Although not brought up around tennis, Barclay found Bond very skilled in his profession, but also a quick learner of the game. Bond worked on giving Cash the skills to remain focused, such as allowing officials to make mistakes without berating them and to build an imaginary cage around himself, where no outside influence could get into his head. At times though with Cash's occasional volatility, even Barclay was not immune from being in the firing line of a verbal spray. It didn't stop him from always enquiring beforehand where his coach would be sitting during each match, a trait of Cash's since he was an 11-year-old.

Barclay was one of the few private tennis coaches of the time to travel exclusively with an individual player. He became well versed at scouting other players' matches on tour and would regularly have valuable tips for Cash before upcoming matches.

Australia had successfully navigated a passage through the early Davis Cup rounds of 1986, defeating New Zealand in Auckland, 4-1 in the first round. That was followed by a 4-1 quarter-final defeat of Great Britain at the All England Club, Wimbledon and a 3-1 semi-final victory over the United States in Brisbane, to set up yet another final against Sweden. Yet again it was played in Melbourne at Kooyong.

In preparation for the Davis Cup final, Quinn put Cash through a series of demanding physical tests to measure his speed, agility, reaction time, endurance, strength, power, muscular endurance, flexibility and body fat. To Quinn's delight, he was tested as faster than Olympic sprinters Ben Johnson and Carl Lewis over 10 metres (using light gates) and was down to 4.2% body fat. His daily training continued to include speed and agility work, as well as tests on his heart rate and recovery. It revealed a remarkably well-conditioned young athlete who, notwithstanding another injury, could endure the ultimate test of tennis fitness, having to play a Davis Cup final which meant playing best of five-set matches in three days – and each set was an advantage set as there were no tiebreakers back then. He was obsessive about his fitness. No stone was left unturned and they trained daily in the lead-up to the Davis Cup final.

Pat Cash joined John Fitzgerald, Paul McNamee and Peter McNamara to take on the in-form Swedish team of Stefan Edberg, Mikael Pernfors and Anders Jarryd. Edberg had been a singles semi-finalist at the recent US Open and Pernfors an unseeded finalist in May at the French Open. They appeared a formidable opponent even without Mats Wilander who was unavailable due to getting married.

The usual tension-packed practice sessions out of the way, Barclay as usual took his front-row seat, having filled Fraser in with any issues regarding Cash that needed concentrating on. Like those around him, he urged the Aussies on at every opportunity.

Cash opened the tie and defeated a nervy Edberg in the first rubber 13-11, 13-11, 6-4 to get Australia off to a great start. A red-hot Pernfors then comfortably defeated McNamee 6-3, 6-1, 6-3 to level the match at one rubber all. Cash and Fitzgerald gave Australia the edge by defeating Edberg and Jarryd in the doubles rubber to give the hosts a 2-1 lead.

Bond could read Cash's mood swings and became deft at sending the occasional signal to him from the stands, oblivious to the umpire. Barclay himself was often scrutinised by officials, allegedly for the same thing. They kept a close eye on him through the regular tour.

In the critical fourth rubber, Pernfors came out firing, this time against Cash. Barclay saw the Swedish number two player hit the ball relentlessly hard for two straight sets and scorch winners from every part of the court. The Aussie looked to his team mates and coach in disbelief, a touch disconsolate, amazed at the level of his opponent's shot making.

From the stands, Barclay and Cash's cup team mates continued to urge him to believe in himself. Cash just holding on, then survived a break point in the opening game of the third set as well as two break points in the third game. A break of the Swede's serve signalled a change in fortunes.

In front of around 12,000 screaming voices, Cash commenced one of the most extraordinary comebacks ever seen in Davis Cup tennis history, Pernfors having had him on the brink. Cash capitalised on the break to take the next two sets.

At the major break Barclay reminded Cash how confident he was of his own physical ability and that he thought Pernfors was just about exhausted at that point. The help that Jeff Bond had given him by imagining himself protected from the screaming Swedish fans was immeasurable.

Two strokes of brilliance in the fifth game of the last set proved pivotal. The first was a running, down-the-line forehand winner, which could have only been played by the quickest of players. It gave Cash a break point. He then sealed the game with a backhand drop volley off a vicious Pernfors cross-court passing attempt.

In claiming victory, Cash's recovery from two sets down in the decisive fourth rubber to win in five sets has gone down in Australian tennis folklore as one of the all-time great Davis Cup comebacks. It gave Australia victory and its 26th Cup. Deep down four-time-winning Cup captain Neale Fraser and Barclay believed Cash was in effect three quarters of the team. "I don't think the Cup has ever been won in greater circumstances than those in which Pat won today," said Fraser.

As the Davis Cup final was played just after Christmas, that left only three weeks till the start of the 1987 Australian Open. This would be the last time the tournament was to be played on grass at Kooyong. From the following year, the newly constructed Flinders Park, situated between the Melbourne Cricket Ground and Olympic Park on the Yarra River, would host future Grand Slam Australian Opens, under auspice of Tennis Australia.

This didn't give Barclay and Cash much time to back up for their country's major tournament. Cash had had a massive workload, playing 140 games of tennis over three Davis Cup rubbers. He had also spent a lot of time working on his serve in the lead-up to the Davis Cup final. Barclay was quietly concerned. He wasn't sure how much Cash had in reserve should he progress through the draw.

Seeded 11th, in defeating Noah in the quarter-final, he injured his shoulder. Overuse and some mis-hit shots had taken its toll. With some outstanding volleying he somehow found a way to defeat number one seed Ivan Lendl in the semi-final, again in four sets, before facing off yet again against Swede Stefan Edberg in the final, who he had defeated only weeks earlier. He took a painkiller to help ease the pain. Although losing the first two sets, he bravely hung in but lost his maiden Grand Slam final in five sets to the brilliant Swede, 3-6, 4-6, 6-3, 7-5, 3-6.

Once the disappointment and dust had settled, Barclay and Cash felt confident about the New Year ahead.

Cash added a third Grand Prix Singles title to his belt in March, defeating fellow Australian Wally Masur in the final of the Lorraine tournament in Nancy, France, 6-2, 6-3, on carpet.

Sustaining a knee injury though, he required a month off following arthroscopic surgery. After a first-round loss in the French Open that left Cash devastated, this inadvertently allowed him, Barclay and the team the opportunity to get to London earlier than expected, in order to set the wheels in motion for their Wimbledon campaign. It had rained incessantly in the lead-up, so arriving ahead of the rest of the field gave Cash extra time for some much-needed training and practice on the grass surface. Ann Quinn believed it was a blessing in disguise.

Hitting every day and putting in solid hours, Barclay thought Cash looked a 'million' dollars. There was, however, a small scare on the eve of Wimbledon. A practice session at Queens saw Cash feel discomfort in his back. Fearing the worst, Barclay and Cash's father organised for the player's Melbourne physiotherapist, David Zuker to make a flying visit to London. Fortunately, it was a false alarm. He was suffering only some muscle stiffness.

Now with three tournament wins on the tough Men's tour, Barclay felt that Cash had proven unequivocally that he could play the game at the highest level, under the most extreme pressure. Winning national titles as a junior, the tough Avvenire Cup in Italy, the Galea Cup, his junior Grand Slam titles, his Davis Cup wins and his first Grand Slam Singles finals appearance could not have laid a better foundation for an attack on the grandest individual trophy of them all – The Championships, Wimbledon.

The Championships, Wimbledon

Wimbledon 1987 began and the quality of the Men's Singles field read like the Who's Who of tennis. Of the top 10 seeds, there were six Grand Slam Singles titleholders – Boris Becker, Ivan Lendl, Mats Wilander, Stefan Edberg, Yannick Noah and Jimmy Connors. Miloslav Mecir had been a runner-up once already and 10th seed, Tim Mayotte, had reached a Grand Slam semi-final twice previously.

Almost any on that list could win the coveted title. Only a decade earlier Bjorn Borg and John McEnroe had duelled for the majority of Grand Slams. Now there were plenty of new contenders on the block.

Pat Cash was seeded 11th for the tournament. He chose to concentrate only on singles because of the potential workload ahead, therefore opting not to play the doubles. Barclay had been keen for him to play both, but having reflected on the previous year's campaign, knew it may have been physically impossible.

Cash's preparation for his Wimbledon tilt had been almost military-like in its precision. Barclay kept a close eye, as every detail was calculated to the exact second to when he stepped onto tennis' hallowed turf.

He ate a high carbohydrate breakfast of specially blended cereals with a low-fat and high-protein content and home-made energy muffins and juice. After breakfast, he embarked on a 45-minute warm-up session of a run, stretches and short, sharp agility and reaction time work with Quinn at Bishops Park, just around the corner from his London home. He would then travel to the club and practise at Aorangi Park, 90 minutes before his first-round match.

Cash then restored his energy with another light meal at the All England Club and Jeff Bond helped relax his mind, particularly with some turmoil that had surfaced on the home front.

Some further inclement weather during the first week at times saw Barclay scour the countryside for a dry grass court to practice on. All papers, TV and media were off limits so he was sheltered from any outside influences. All things considered, Barclay believed he could make a real impact on the tournament.

After a first-round straight sets 6-0, 6-3, 6-2 win against American Marciel Freeman, Cash set up a potentially tricky second round against great mate and fellow Aussie Davis Cup player Paul McNamee. After a nervous start and long first set, Cash beat his older compatriot, again in straight sets 7-5, 6-4, 6-2. On the same day, top seed and reigning champion Boris Becker was sensationally defeated by Aussie compatriot and journeyman Peter Doohan in the second round. Quietly, the result gave Barclay great encouragement. However, he didn't allow himself or Cash to get too far ahead of themselves. They stayed in the moment and concentrated solely on the next match.

Overcoming the tall, awkward Dutchman, Michiel Schapers, in four sets 7-6, 6-2, 2-6, 6-4, albeit having some temperamental moments, a fourth-round encounter loomed against a genuine title contender, left-handed Frenchman, Guy Forget. In what Barclay regarded was Cash's best match of the fortnight, the Australian defeated Forget 6-2, 6-3, 6-4. As Forget walked past Barclay after the match, he paused briefly, telling the coach that it didn't matter who Cash played, he could beat anyone left in the field.

Now at the business end of the tournament, Cash captured two major scalps, both remarkably in straight sets. Moving beautifully, he defeated third seed Mats Wilander in the quarter-final 6-3, 7-5, 6-4, then in the semi-final, the 35-year-old wily seventh seed American legend, Jimmy Connors 6-4, 6-4, 6-1. Barclay had often watched and greatly admired Connors' drive during every point he played but knew only too well his intimidatory tactics. He also knew that Cash's practice sessions with Aussie left-hander Brad Drewett before the Connors match were invaluable.

Ian Barclay's star pupil had made the Wimbledon Men's Singles Final.

It brought a match up with the number-one-ranked player in the world and number two seed for the tournament, Czech, Ivan Lendl. There was no love lost between the two and Cash relished the thought of taking on his opponent. As Barclay remarked, "Lendl was not exactly the most liked guy on the circuit. He could get under the skin of a lot of the other guys. He and Pat almost came to blows in an altercation in Italy a couple of years earlier over a pair of Pat's new running shoes that Lendl had jokingly tried to destroy in the players' locker room."

Barclay knew what Cash was up against in Lendl but felt he was in with a real chance. The Czech player was desperate to win the cherished title and made it known publicly he would gladly exchange any one of his three French or two US Opens for just one Wimbledon crown.

So focused was Cash on the task ahead, not even Prime Minister Bob Hawke could get a telephone call through with best wishes to the young Australian in the lead-up to the final. Quinn had him in peak condition, psychologist Jeff Bond helped him handle his nerves, anxiety and tension before the biggest match of his tennis life and fellow Aussie Darren Cahill had warmed him up on the practice court.

Barclay never too far from the action, instructed Cahill on how to play, mirroring what he anticipated Lendl would do.

British Prime Minister Margaret Thatcher and the late Princess Diana of Wales were in the Royal Box to watch the final.

Tactically wise, Barclay had told his charge that he thought Lendl was a bit brick handed at the net and that whatever happened, when Lendl did come to the net, to make sure he made him play every volley, and where possible get the ball low to his feet. The Czech, he believed, would make mistakes off it. Barclay knew that in the modern game, if a player had one weakness, the better opponents could cut it to pieces. Mindful of how success in matches is based around winning the big points, he reminded Cash of the importance of capturing the first point of each game.

Like the playing of a broken record, Barclay's simple, basic messages to Cash that he had drummed into him throughout his junior career were being played out on the grandest of stages. Cash had always trusted his coach. In front of 12,500 spectators Cash returned serve positively from the outset of the match. Ivan Lendl was under early pressure.

Lendl was missing first serves. He served mainly to the Cash backhand, which the Aussie returned superbly, either for outright winners or to put Lendl back on the back foot. When the Czech did venture to the net, his volleys were executed with little confidence. Cash would often roll the ball to his feet. It then set him up for his beautifully disguised top-spin lob. It proved pivotal in the first set.

Cash himself was playing flawless grass court serve and volley tennis. He and Barclay had practised this for hours. The Australian locked away the first set 7-6, seven points to five in the tiebreaker in 73 minutes, albeit on his sixth set point. Cash served so well himself that he didn't lose a single point on serve in the second set. On his serve, Lendl continued serving to Cash's backhand. Such was the level of the returns, Lendl forced himself to go for even more on his serve, ultimately making more errors.

The start of the third set saw Cash have a small lapse after having had an incredible run on serve. He missed some volleys, which resulted in him dropping his first service game of the match. Lendl believed he still had a chance, as long as he could just hang in.

Temporary nerves were quickly quelled, helped by Bond's teachings. Two great Cash returns on the first two points of Lendl's next service game put the pressure straight back on to his opponent.

Serving at 5-3 and still with a break, Lendl reverted back to serving to the Cash backhand and duly paid the price.

Cash broke and was back on track. He served out the final game of the match to love. He had held 10 out of 16 service games to love.

Two hours and 45 minutes from when it had begun, he had danced his way to a straight sets 7-6, 6-2, 7-5 win, thus realising his dream of lifting tennis' ultimate individual trophy.

The ultimate prize – 1987 champions Barclay and Cash embrace in the stands after victory over Ivan Lendl

Lendl remarked Cash had played great tennis, barely missing any first serves and acknowledged the Australian had played too well, particularly paying attention to his athleticism and strategy. "When I saved several break points in the third set, it was the only time he had a letdown when he missed three easy volleys. He put so much pressure on my own serve."

The young Aussie, who often liked to do things differently, wanted to share the moment with those in his team that had helped him and to show the world in the process.

In an historic and unprecedented move, after shaking hands at the end of the match, Cash precariously climbed up into the stands, over spectators and up to the players' box. For a brief moment Barclay's heart was in his mouth, as there was a 30-foot drop beneath the box down to the standing room only area. Cash warmly embraced his all-important team, his father Patrick, his uncle Brian, sister Renee, girlfriend Anne-Britt, fitness advisor Quinn, psychologist Bond and of course Barclay. Player and coach then embraced. A hug from each and then words from Cash to his mentor. "We fucking did it, Barkers, we fucking did it!" It could well have summed up what both men had felt deep down for all the years and hours of work they had put in and towards those who had doubted them since the Australian first came to prominence as a young teenager.

In his autobiography *Uncovered*, of Barclay Cash said, "I wouldn't have won that day but for him. Indeed, I probably wouldn't even have been playing the tournament. Without doubt he was the most important contributor to my career." As far as he was concerned, it was he and Barclay. "I was Barker's creation and I'm sure that for him to see his creation come through to win a Wimbledon title was absolutely huge for him. I still pinch myself sometimes and think how did I win that? Without Barkers I wouldn't have done it. It was such a big day for us all."

While Barclay was in the players' box during Cash's singles final, the rest of the Barclays and friends had set up camp at the family Park Orchards house ready to urge team Cash on. They were going to party, come what may. And party they did, in typical Australian Rules Grand Final-like spirit. After Cash secured match point, the house went crazy. No one got to bed till 3 am the following morning.

For Barclay, two words summed up his feelings once Pat Cash had achieved his boyhood dream – 'total elation'. The coach, who had promised himself he would loyally stick with the young boy through thick and thin from the moment he realised the potential he had before him at the Heatherdale Tennis Club 11 years earlier, was now in his own seventh heaven.

His words to wife Jackie during the 1980 junior MATCH tour regarding Cash's potential and future prospects had come true. Over the course of Cash's career, there had been plenty of thick and just as much thin. Injuries, fines, media run-ins, fatherhood and the like were a part of the rollercoaster that was Pat Cash.

Barclay revealed some inner feelings after the victory. "I was told I would never make a tennis player out of Pat Cash. People said I had never been a Davis Cup player and I had never won Wimbledon so how could he possibly do it under my guidance? I'd had success with other students in national and international tournaments but still received a lot of rubbishing. Some of my peers made statements I'm sure they regret now. We have proved them all wrong. If I had 1000 pupils, it's a fair chance only one would ever possibly make it to the top. Pat has done it. He's the best competitor I've ever seen. He just has this amazing willpower to win. He doesn't know how to take a step back and has accepted every challenge I've ever put before him. His temper and his ability go hand in hand. Today my dream came true. From his back injury that sidelined him for months at the end of 1985, he grew up overnight. It was the year he really matured. Although the injury was frustrating for all of us, it was the first time he had had the chance to appreciate his family and friends. He was down then and people were saying he was finished. But all he said to me was, "Here we go again, Barkers, we'll show em!"

"Watching him win today was the most wonderful feeling I've ever had in the game. I thought he played the perfect second set in which he didn't lose a point on serve. He served and returned serve brilliantly. He has done monumental things for his country and it goes back long before Davis Cup, to our MATCH trips to Europe. All I could ever do with Pat was ask him to give his all, something any coach can only hope for. When I saw him running up those stands to the players' box, I thought for God's sake don't get another injury." At the end of the match, Barclay turned to Lendl's coach, fellow Australian Tony Roche and spoke of the benefit Australian tennis could get from Cash's win. "What a wonderful day for all our kids, all those kids with dreams."

Tennis Australia officials subsequently predicted a boom in Australian tennis. They believed the Australian's success would help restore the country's tennis pride that had seemingly wilted since John Newcombe in 1971 and Evonne Cawley in 1980, who last won Wimbledon Singles crowns. They believed that grassroots player participation and corporate sponsorship could receive a significant boost, similar to the effect to that of German tennis stars Boris Becker and Steffi Graf.

Barclay's great mate Will Coghlan believed that it took Pat Cash's win at Wimbledon for the governing body of tennis in Australia to finally take some action and start to seriously think about the next generation of young players coming through. Identifying talent, putting much-needed funds, facilities and programs in place to help develop young Australian players finally got on the national tennis agenda.

Barclay though, believed it was short lived. For a while tennis boomed and there were plenty of black-and-white-chequered headbands worn on tennis courts. But with other sports competing heavily in the marketplace as well, it had only limited impact. It would take Pat Rafter and his success in the late 1990s to once again regenerate a strong interest across the board in the game.

Barclay's protégé had risen to become one of Australia's highest profile sportsmen, sitting alongside golfing great Greg Norman and Olympic long-distance runner Robert de Castella. Now ranked world number seven, sudden fame now left Cash as prey to the prying world of the sporting media, which would seek a closer and more permanent insight into his professional and private life. How Barclay and Cash handled the off-court side of his life would perhaps be the single biggest test of the coach and Australia's newest Wimbledon champion and sporting millionaire.

Post Wimbledon

Not long after, Cash and girlfriend Anne-Britt were expectant parents again, this time to future daughter, Mia Karin. Further celebrations were again held, back at the coach's house in Park Orchards on Barclay's and Cash's return to Melbourne. It didn't take long for the coach to climb onto his soapbox once the beer and champagne started to flow. "As the night grew older the 'Barclay bullshit' got louder," said Andrew Crossman. "It was an exciting time, the drinks were on and Barkers was in his element. Stories got taller, fabrication grew thicker and at one point assistant coach Rocky Loccisano asked, "Hey, Barkers, don't tell me, after having all the hostesses around your little finger, you offered to fly the plane home from London as well." The place erupted and Barclay was revelling. It was often said by those close to him that in his excitement, if one divided what he said by half, then half again, you would then get close to the truth of the matter."

Barclay was just as proud of Cash every time he returned to Australia. Unpretentious, he became just one of the boys again, mixing among his local mates that he had grown up with. Cash and Dean Barclay were long-standing friends. When they got together with their tennis mates, they were as thick as thieves.

Cash was given a brand new Porsche to try out. Ian suspected the boys took the car out and burnt off all the tyres on the local freeway. They would regularly go to see their favourite rock bands, wherever they played, with entry often courtesy of Cash's elevated status. Legendary hard rock band Iron Maiden was a favourite of Pat, Dean and others. Being music enthusiasts, they eventually met some of the band members and occasionally got up to accompany them on stage, which at different times could be anywhere around the world. Barclay sometimes ventured into some of the nightclubs himself.

As almost everyone smoked 'the funny stuff', the coach admitted one couldn't help but get high, such was the waft of thick smoke in the air. Barclay found it incredible how many superstars from various walks of life patronised the club scene.

Music works in funny ways. At one point, Barclay was training on a beach in the Bahamas with rock band Iron Maiden's lead singer, Steve Harris, helping him to get fit, when suddenly they bumped into Mick Jagger and members of the legendary band, the Rolling Stones. Harris had been asked to gather up a team for a game of soccer for charity. Introducing Barclay to the small, lithe, fragile-looking Jagger, Harris asked whether the Stones would join the team to play. Jagger replied that he didn't play soccer; he only played the brutal, bruising game of rugby. Barclay nearly wet himself laughing. Members of Iron Maiden often took up positions in the front row at Flushing Meadows to watch some of Cash's matches. The crowd would erupt, not always just to applaud the great tennis.

Pat Cash was based in London and keen for Barclay to be close by. After Wimbledon, Barclay and Cash's mother Dorothy started looking at prospective houses.

Barclay knew that in order for Cash to gain direct entry into the end-of-year Masters Play Off event at Madison Square Garden, New York, featuring the top eight players in the world, his last chance was to play the South African Open in Johannesburg. Commitment to Davis Cup in Australia had left him short of points up till now. As well, the financial inducement couldn't be resisted.

Cash's entry into the South African tournament had the coach's home telephone in Park Orchards ringing hot. There were accusations and personal threats to the family from those involved in the anti-apartheid movement, who opposed any support of such events in the troubled country. In their hotel in Johannesburg, media calls to Cash needed to be diverted to Barclay's room, simply to get them off the player's back.

Early on in the tournament, Cash had plenty of racquets on hand, but he had difficulty when breaking strings. Each time he sent a racquet off to be restrung, it came back at a different tension than what had been requested, causing both player and coach great frustration. Barclay lost count of how many times he went backwards and forwards to the restringing room until it was done correctly.

In the final, Cash played American Brad Gilbert in front of a packed house. Such was the battle for seats, Barclay at one stage eyed off a girl on the opposite side of the court being forcibly pushed off the end of her seat and down onto a pavement, injuring herself badly. In a match where Gilbert soft balled Cash and attempted to slow the game down with his typically thought-out tactics, the Aussie came from two sets to one down to defeat the American 7-6, 4-6, 2-6, 6-0, 6-1 in the final, winning the last 11 games straight, to secure the last Masters position.

Resentment of Cash competing in South Africa further filtered over into the 1988 Australian Open where protesters continued to vent their anger during Cash's first-round centre court match. Many black-coloured tennis balls were thrown onto the court as a form of protest.

Ironically, Ian and Jackie went back to South Africa the following year. They visited some of the poorest cities, such as Soweto and Stellenbosch, where Barclay conducted junior clinics. They wanted to bring two teenage children, one coloured and one non-coloured, back to Australia for a short period of more intensive coaching. Over the years, it had resonated deep inside Barclay to help some of the world's most underprivileged children get a chance to improve their lives through tennis. Cash supported the idea and was prepared to fully fund the project.

However, this ultimately proved impossible, as one high-standing, then member of the Australian Olympic Committee was very anti anyone visiting from South Africa for such a purpose. The government refused to give any child a visa. Barclay received several further threatening telephone calls until he decided to abandon the idea for good.

Barclay's increased amount of time spent on the professional tennis tour meant he could be away from home for months on end. The Barclay children had even less of their father's time, but realised this was the price they had to pay for their father being a full-time professional tennis coach. Proud of their father's success to date, it gradually fuelled each of their own desires to travel the world.

Barclay decided this was a good time to take the entire family on their first overseas trip together to the US. While there, he took on a part-time coaching role with a young satellite-level player ranked around 150 in the world. The Barclays stayed with the host family. Toni-Ann recalled that, with all five of them staying in the one place, it didn't take long for the fireworks and arguments to erupt. "The hosts were flabbergasted, having never seen anything or anyone like the Barclay family in full conflict mode. They laughingly suggested they ought to adopt me and leave the remainder of the family to themselves."

Pat Cash, seeded fourth, made the final of the Australian Open in 1988 for the second year in a row.

This was the first year the Open was played at Melbourne's new National Tennis Centre on an equally new rubberised hardcourt surface called Rebound Ace, underneath a retractable roof. A quarter-final win over Dutchman Michiel Schapers matched Cash up yet again against Ivan Lendl in the semi-final. A five-sets win made it three successive victories in Grand Slams against one of his most disliked adversaries.

Mats Wilander, the ever-consistent Swede, was his opponent in the final. From the stands Barclay saw one of the most topsy-turvy matches he had ever seen. A couple of rain delays played a part in a series of momentum shifts throughout the match. One critical moment deep into the match was when Cash hit a perfect cross-court volley, only for the normally double-hand-backhanded Wilander to race outside the doubles line and hit an unbelievable one-handed backhand back around the net post for a winner on the singles sideline. Cash went down fighting in his hometown Grand Slam to the Swede in five sets 3-6, 7-6 (3) 6-3, 1-6, 6-8.

Disappointingly, this would be his last real chance to secure his home Grand Slam title.

Barclay's Ultimate Competitor

In Barclay's mind, perhaps Pat Cash's best Davis Cup performance came in February of 1988 in Australia's first-round away tie against Mexico on clay in the melting pot of Mexico City, played at a plush country club.

There were very few Australians there outside the team to witness the contest. Barclay had long hailed the Thursdays before a cup tie as 'bad Thursday' because he knew it was the time when Cash would vent all his frustrations and anxieties out on the practice court. But this was important too as Cash needed to be in the right frame of mind and ready to go come game day. With a bit of luck, by the time matches came around, he still had some racquets to use.

The pre-match nerves in Mexico were again evident and a few more of Cash's racquets went past their used-by date during his practice sessions with squad member Tasmanian Simon Youl on 'bad Thursday' out on Court 19, away from the public eye. Captain, Neale Fraser asked Barclay how he thought Pat might perform. Practice out of the way, the coach said he believed Cash was well and truly ready to play.

Wally Masur lost two heartbreaking singles matches, the first against Mexican Francisco Marciel, the other in the reverse match to Leonardo Lavalle. Cash accounted for Lavalle comfortably in his opening rubber. Masur warned Cash that Marciel had tried to intimidate him during his match, and to be wary of his tactics when his turn came to play.

The entire tie was a turbulent affair. Cash and John Fitzgerald played the doubles against Lavalle and Jorge Lorzano, who was ranked number one doubles player in the world at the time.

Neale Fraser sent Barclay and Simon Youl into the stands to make sure the line calls were okay. If they weren't, they were to give a signal and Fraser would challenge the umpire. After the Aussies won the first set, Fitzgerald hit a poor half volley over the net early in the second. Lorzano charged in and drilled Cash with the next shot, then leant over the net with his fist raised in celebration and screamed, "Yeah!" Youl leaned across to Barclay and said of the Mexican, "This guy is dead."

Quietly incensed, Cash waited a couple of games for his chance. Soon after a framed Lorzano shot allowed Cash to unleash a stinging drive volley that landed straight into the midriff of his opponent. Lorzano went down like a ton of bricks. Cash put his own fist over the net and returned the compliment, yelling, "Yeah!"

Keeping Masur's cautionary words in mind, Cash went out to play the tie's deciding fifth rubber against Marciel. The Mexican deliberately drilled a short backhand straight at him during the hit-up. Cash's answer was swift. He took one of the balls he was holding and hit a squash forehand shot directly at Marciel as he turned and headed back to the baseline. The ball narrowly missed the Mexican's head as it continued on an upward trajectory, slamming into the backdrop. Some reverse psychology appeared to occur as it was the Mexican who started to look intimidated.

Barclay was proud that his prize charge would in no way be stood over. Barclay, knowing how fired-up Australia's number one weapon was, warned him not to get too close to the Mexican player's box at any stage when collecting balls from the ball kids for fear of possible verbal or physical retaliation. In the final throes of the match, Cash could not help himself. On match point he deliberately meandered up underneath the player's box and while playing with his racquet strings, collected the balls, at the same time giving his adversaries a quiet mouthful. He then stepped up to serve the winning ace.

Barclay and the rest of the Davis Cup team copped constant abuse throughout the tie. They were jeered, spat at, and had coins thrown at them regularly throughout the match. With the tie won with Cash's second singles victory over Marciel, the team was walking off the court congratulating each other when they turned around to find Barclay wasn't behind them.

Barclay had been hit by a coin on the top of the eye and was busy chasing down the spectator who had thrown the missile.

A short time later back in the locker room, a sweaty, angry, cursing and bloodied Barclay strode in, only to be confronted with a teary Davis Cup official Tony Ryan, explaining they had a potential international incident on their hands. To compound the problems, local police were trying to arrest, charge and extort money from Wally Masur, who had allegedly pushed the son of the club's president into the team's hotel pool after his second singles loss.

Barclay to this day still bears a small scar, courtesy of that direct hit. Of all the incidents Barclay recalled, that was the worst crowd behaviour he had ever witnessed anywhere around the world. They had come at the Aussies from everywhere.

Barclay ranked the effort in Mexico equal to, if not above Cash's come-from-behind, five-set win against Sweden's Mikael Pernfors in the 1986 Davis Cup final. "Pat was just so mentally tough. From a young age he had this amazing inner desire to be the fittest player in the world. Nothing would get between him and what he was focused towards. He believed he was so fit, that he could come back from literally any position to win any match. It is also amazing what his mind was capable of doing."

Davis Cup was the team competition that in Barclay's mind stood above all else in the world of tennis. Cash held similar sentiment and when it came around each year, it endeared the public towards the young Aussie.

Barclay's favourite memories of the Davis Cup campaigns were the comradeship between the Australian players. "If they hadn't been the closest of friends, the Cup ties brought them together.

"Cash was always the youngest and McNamee, Wally Masur, John Fitzgerald and McNamara all took Pat under their wing. If I asked anything of the boys for Pat, they would do it." Often misled by the media, barring injury, he would always step up when selected to play for his country. The biggest issue for Barclay was that Cash generally needed to win his three matches each tie as there was no player highly enough ranked to be guaranteed of winning the second singles.

During the lead-up to the 1989 Australian Open, another great competitor in the making, a young 17-year-old American called Pete Sampras, arrived in Australia with his elder brother.

Sampras sought out Barclay for some assistance to his game prior to his first Grand Slam event Down Under. He had got to know Barclay from the coach's time spent in the United States.

It was Christmas time. Typical of Barclay, he thought it would be nice for the brothers to spend it with a couple of Heatherdale Tennis Club families rather than by themselves in a lonely hotel room. Lunch was had at the Loccisano family home followed by dinner at the Bland family home. At lunch, one family member flippantly asked Sampras if he thought he could ever reach number one in the world. The young American shyly remarked how he didn't know because of how tough a road he thought it was to get to the top. Less than two years later he won his first Grand Slam Singles title at the US Open. Little did they know Pete Sampras would go on to win 14 Grand Slam Singles titles.

Time off the Tour

Barclay and wife Jackie had not long moved into a three-bedroom house in Merton Park, a suburb of Wimbledon.

A fourth-round loss to Edberg at the 1989 Australian Open, combined with a less than memorable first-round away Davis Cup loss to Austria saw Pat Cash reach a significant low in his tennis career.

His relationship with his Norwegian girlfriend and now mother of two, Anne-Britt, had reached breaking point. They split up. To add salt to Cash's wound, he ruptured his Achilles tendon in April while playing in a lucrative tournament in Tokyo.

The injury allowed Barclay time to play some more tennis in Germany during 1989 with Rocky Loccisano, who had stayed on in Europe and at the time was based at the Babcock Tennis Club in Oberhausen, both playing and coaching. Together, they entered the Men's Open Doubles at the Niederrhein regional state championships. The organisers didn't know Barclay and strongly suggested to Loccisano that the 51-year-old coach enter the Seniors' age event, so as not to embarrass himself against the best players from around the region. Little did they know of his doubles expertise.

Barclay felt like a punching bag as round by round opponents relentlessly fired heavy groundstrokes at him when at the net.

They won four matches to reach the final, where they held a match point, only to finish runners-up in three sets against a pair more than half the coach's age. Barclay won the Over 45 Singles title.

Like his MATCH junior teams in the late 1970s and early 1980s, he had learnt the craft of playing Europeans on their own surface. In singles, he became more reserved with his normal serve and volley strategy. He needed to remain on the baseline for longer periods, defend strongly and hit more shots in order to construct and win points. This was particularly difficult in Germany, where the rain could come in from the North Sea, the balls became heavier and winners at times near impossible to hit. Barclay felt the European clay was softer than the traditional en tout cas surface that he had grown up on in Melbourne. "You slid on dust rather than ball bearings and the clay wasn't quite as taxing on the body. For me clay has always been the ideal surface on which to learn the game, because of its true bounce and slower speed."

Barclay was presented with another opportunity to continue working during Pat Cash's eight-month hiatus from the tour. He innocently bumped into British National Coach and Davis Cup Captain, Australian Warren Jacques. When asked what he was up to, Barclay said not much. Jacques asked if he was interested in spending some time working with members of the British Davis Cup squad. Barclay responded positively. When the Lawn Tennis Association (LTA) offered him a short-term contract, he jumped at it. The group included tour players Andrew Castle, Nick Brown and James Turner. Barclay knew all three from the professional tournament scene.

Castle, a professional of four years, had held a career-high world singles ranking of 80 and at times held his country's number one ranking. He had one tour singles and two doubles runner-up finishes when he met Barclay. He had only known Barclay as the silver-headed guy who coached Pat Cash on the tour, but remembers being in a hotel room in Indianapolis in 1987 while playing in the US Clay court championships and seeing the Aussie win Wimbledon. "It delighted me no end to see him win that title," said Castle, whom he had ironically played in his Davis Cup debut for Britain the previous year in the reverse singles of a quarter-final tie with Australia. Although while still one of his country's best players, in his own words, "By the time Barkers came along for us, unfortunately I was well towards the end of my career both physically and mentally."

At 27 years of age, Brown had come back to the professional tour after five years in semi-retirement. A relative late bloomer from the north of England, he had won the 1980 Under 21 Years British Championships and then the Men's event in 1983. However, he had scaled back playing on the tour, firstly because of lack of money and secondly because there was no support system to fall back on through the LTA during hard times for players.

During that time, he ventured to Belgium and France to coach, played club tennis, competed in some money tournaments on the weekends and then took on a carer's role for his elderly parents. He spent some time coaching young English prospect Tim Henman, kept practising, then won the British closed doubles championships, which led to him getting wild cards into Wimbledon and other tournaments. From there Brown re-entered the pro tour and not long after, he met Barclay. He was ranked around 600 in the world.

Essentially self-taught, Turner had never been a part of any national squad until he started beating some of the higher-ranked British players at around 18 years of age. He had turned professional in 1985, combined with Castle to make the semi-finals of Bristol in 1986 and had a fine win over world top 10 player, Yugoslav Slobodan Zivojinovic in the first round of the 1988 Stella Artois tournament at the Queen's Club. Prior to linking up with Barclay, he had been runner-up in May the same year in a challenger event in Johannesburg.

Barclay told the three players to meet him at a local hotel to discuss the immediate future. The effervescent Castle replied he first needed to fix up his fiancée's outrageous telephone bill, and then he would be straight over.

The three-month stint with the British Davis Cup players coincided with the northern hemisphere grass court season, which started about five weeks before the start of Wimbledon. Barclay worked closely alongside the squad's Bosnian trainer, Hak Hravek. Barclay noted Hravek's unique ability to just look into his athlete's eyes and decipher their fitness level. He could determine whether they were sleep deprived or if they had any drugs or alcohol in their system. He was also tough on his players and believed they would almost need a broken leg not to get out on the court and compete.

Barclay liked this attitude and took on his new role with energy and gusto, working the Brits hard. The squad was on the practice court five hours a day and often nagged to death by their new coach, in particular about the tactical inadequacies of their games. The players lapped up his knowledge. Brown and Turner found that Barclay completely opened up their eyes with his coaching methods. He taught them simple things about the game they had never learned. Adjustments were made to Brown's serve, volley and in particular his court awareness.

Said Brown, "Barkers constantly promoted our positive attributes, but just as easily gave us a bollocking if we didn't come up to the mark. Meeting Barclay in essence changed my life. He gave me the opportunity to gain so much knowledge and belief in myself that I had never had before. Age didn't matter so much to him. It was a matter of how much you wanted it, your effort levels and desire."

A week before Wimbledon there was the tournament in Bristol for which Brown received another wild card. He made the final, defeating 1991 Wimbledon Champion Michael Stich of Germany along the way, only to lose to another highly ranked German, Eric Jelen at the final hurdle, in a tough three-set match. Barclay was courtside for each of Brown's matches. He quizzed Brown afterwards regarding what appeared to be a lapse in concentration part way through the match. Brown mentioned that he had been consumed by thoughts of upcoming divorce proceedings.

Barclay reflected on how someone like Jeff Bond could have been a valuable asset at that time.

Immediately after Wimbledon, Barclay took the squad to South East Asia to play in a number of lower-ranked money tournaments on the challenger tour. He believed they needed to get plenty of matches, as well as the opportunity to attain important points to help lift their rankings. The trip took in Kuala Lumpur, Jakarta, Singapore and Hong Kong. They were quickly on the practice court in Kuala Lumpur, but struggled to come to terms with the heat and humidity.

The best the team could achieve were quarter-final results for both Castle and Turner in the singles where they lost to journeymen Australian Neil Borwick and New Zealand's Steven Guy respectively. Barclay knew the Aussies hated being beaten by the Poms. As top seeds, Nick Brown and Andrew Castle reached the semi-final of the doubles. In the second week in Jakarta, Barclay and his Brits again came across several young touring Australians including future Grand Slam doubles champion Todd Woodbridge. The group's accommodation was average at best. They stayed at one of the Hilton hotels which was surrounded by razor wire. In what was a particularly strong field, Turner defeated Woodbridge in a quarter-final, then Castle in a semi-final.

Nick Brown was having some issues with his movement. He had developed a rather nasty split in his skin, underneath the ball of his foot. The constant heat and perspiration had Brown feeling he was always moving on water. Barclay bandaged his foot before each match. During an injury time-out, Barclay managed the wound using Band-Aids. Barclay explained the seriousness of the injury to Brown and told him that he could well be finished and may need to get back to London. Brown retorted, "Barkers, you're the one who told us all it didn't matter how injured we were, we still had to play." Barclay told him if the wound became infected in the environment they were living in, he wouldn't have a foot to play on. Remarkably, Brown got through his side of the draw, then defeated compatriot Turner in the final in straight sets.

Without much time to celebrate, the group went off to the $50,000 Singapore event the same evening. One of Barclay's friends worked for a major beer company and knew of the coach's impending arrival. On entering their hotel room, Barclay and Brown found not only the bar fridge stocked full with the local *Tiger* brand beer, but the cupboards as well. It was an opportune time to celebrate Brown's Jakarta win. The next day in stifling heat, Turner, while comfortably accounting for his opening match of the new tournament, heard a voice from the back of the stands, "Come on, Jimmy, hurry up, we've got beer to drink." The match done and won, both coach and player disappeared from the cauldron of the tennis court back to the cooler confines of the hotel room to try and lighten the load of some of the sponsor's refreshing product.

Brown's foot injury was significantly severe enough for him to pull out of the singles. Injuries to the squad made Barclay question whether he had been overworking his players. Castle, though, came away with the doubles title with Australian Broderick Dyke. "The boys kept standing up. They just wanted to learn all the time and work hard for me." Barclay's enjoyable three-month tenure finished at their final tournament in Hong Kong where a fitter Brown reached the singles semi-final. Brown was convinced his association with Barclay helped him go from his previous low ranking to 145 in the world, his best ever singles ranking. His doubles ranking was now at 42.

After Hong Kong, Barclay resumed with Pat Cash, who was back in training. The British boys remained in contact with Barclay. Nick Brown went down to Australia for the end-of-year summer circuit and stayed at the coach's Park Orchards home and practised with Cash and others on the backyard court each day. The Brit had become very close to both Ian and Jackie and like Cash and other pupils before him, the tennis guru had become somewhat of a second father to him.

With Barclay again at the helm, Cash returned to the tournament scene and won the doubles in Sydney with another Aussie, Mark Kratzman. Now with a ranking of around 600 in the world, Cash went to Korea for the Seoul Open, but had to qualify for the main draw. He made it to the final, only to lose to Austrian Davis Cup player Alex Antonitsch 6-7, 3-6. He then exacted revenge the following week by winning the Hong Kong Open, defeating the Austrian 6-3, 6-4.

Although playing most of the remainder of the year, Cash had mediocre results by his standards, but still managed to help guide Australia into another Davis Cup final, this time against the United States, in St Petersburg, Florida, held at the end of the year. The American team included Andre Agassi, Michael Chang and doubles specialists Jim Pugh and Rick Leach. Disappointingly, the team lost the first three rubbers and with it the tie. A gloomy mood hung over the camp. The final though, happened to fall on Barclay's birthday. A friend of Cash's decided to brighten up the mood surrounding the team. He organised a couple of female strippers to be smuggled into the Aussies' locker room at the conclusion of the match. Neale Fraser got Barclay inside, shut the doors on the other dignitaries and the players propped the coach on a chair in the middle of the floor while the two girls danced a striptease around him. "It was the first time I think I've ever seen Barkers so embarrassed that he didn't know which way to look," said Cash, who stood on the door and kept out officials from both countries so as his coach could have some fun, on an otherwise uneventful day.

The Split

By now Pat Cash had a new lady in his life and in July of 1990 married Brazilian girlfriend Emily Bendit. Dean Barclay was best man and then became godfather to their twin boys Jett and Shannon.

Cash's tennis showed little sign of improvement. Gloomily, Barclay saw in his star pupil a player the shadow of his former self, happy to be almost anywhere but on a tennis court and playing accordingly. The combination of a new marriage and family demands, rankings drop, niggling injuries and declining motivation levels came to a head after his second-round Wimbledon loss to Frenchman Thierry Champion.

The coach let his observations be known to his Grand Slam titleholder. Not long after, the Barclay-Cash tennis association of 18 years, which had seen them both experience the ultimate in highs and lows of the professional tennis game, was over.

The media frenzy went into overdrive. Brad Barclay was woken in the early hours of the morning back at the family's Park Orchards home to the continual ringing of the telephone. A steady stream of reporters and journalists were hot on the trail of a scoop in relation to his father's sudden split with Cash. Brad knew little of what had developed overseas and even less that his voice was about to be broadcast on national radio around the country over the following few hours.

The split took an emotional toll on Barclay. He had given so much of his professional and personal life to Australia's number one player. From the young boy of 11 years of age, who years earlier had asked his coach whether one day he thought he could win Wimbledon, in Cash Barclay believed he had the ultimate competitor. The same player who accumulated a mountain of state, national and international junior titles. The same player, who over an eight-year period played his heart out for his country and for his coach each time he stepped on court anywhere around the world, and who had amassed a most enviable 31-10 win/loss Davis Cup record. The same player who had reached a career-high singles ranking of four in singles and six in doubles on the ATP Tour amongst some of the world's finest. Barclay had not only been his coach, but had been like a second father, advisor, and just as importantly, a great mate.

Word spread around the tennis world. Barclay was presented with two genuine offers from prominent players to both coach and travel the world with them. Argentinian beauty Gabriella Sabbatini was one. A multiple tour singles winner, she won the US Open Women's Singles in 1990, having already been a finalist there in 1988. She was also a finalist at Wimbledon in 1991. The other was from Frenchman Cedric Pioline, twice Grand Slam finalist at both the 1993 US and Wimbledon in 1997. Both were outstanding players, consistently ranked in the top 10 in the world.

Brad Barclay believed his father could well have set himself up for life if he had accepted one or both offers. Having been on the road for so many years with Cash, the coach was reluctant to go down the same path, not sure whether he could do it all over again. He gave both offers due consideration as they came up, but reneged on both. Brad still thought he could easily link up with a big company such as the International Management Group (IMG) or even set up his own tennis academy, in much the same manner as the American entrepreneur Nick Bollittierri. His father was never that interested.

On a somewhat happier note for Barclay, Brit Nick Brown had his best singles result at Wimbledon where he defeated future champion and 10th seed Goran Ivanisevic in four sets in the second round. Barclay had given Brown several tips on how to play the enigmatic Croatian, in particular, not to allow him to hit running passing shots, but to play the ball back behind him where possible to get him off balance. Brown also used his much-improved volley to advantage, the shot he and Barclay had spent hours working on. Barclay recalled how the modestly ranked Brit arrived at SW19 each day on the back of Polish friend Victor Archutowski's Harley Davidson motorbike.

Not long after, Brown decided to leave the circuit for good. Based in Cambridge, he opted to take up coaching a squad of young players, not long out of the junior ranks. He knew he could call on Barclay where necessary to help out and provide another set of eyes to help monitor their progress. He offered himself up to assist Barclay if ever required.

In the interim period, Barclay headed back Down Under. He lent a hand to leading Australian female player Rachel McQuillan in her preparation for the final Grand Slam championship of the year, the US Open.

While at home he decided to offer up his coaching services to Tennis Australia. With an already vast grassroots coaching background behind him, together with an envious record in developing state, national and international junior champions from within his own country, Barclay had put together an outstanding coaching

CV. One thought he would have been much sought after and welcomed anywhere.

Unbelievably the sport's national body didn't come back with any job offers.

Deep down, Barclay felt a lingering resentment in some quarters towards himself, the success he'd had with Cash and his well-known anti-establishment views. It possibly influenced the 'not-wanted' sign put up in front of him.

Geoff Stone, father of daughter Carolyn, who had trained under Barclay at Heatherdale in his Wednesday afternoon junior squad during the 1980s, had closely followed the coach's journey, to the point where he was courtside to watch the coach play back in the 1985 ITF 45's world event at Kooyong. Stone was both President of the Blackburn South Tennis Club and its delegate to Tennis Victoria's Council. Having a strong grasp of grassroots club tennis himself, he fully understood the time, passion and effort Barclay had made in developing his players and the game itself. He knew how valuable an asset Barclay could have been to the future of Australian junior tennis at the time. He was dumbstruck by Tennis Australia's snub of the coach whose credentials, he believed, were second to none.

Long-time pupil and assistant coach to Barclay, Rocky Loccisano assumed the role of hitting partner and coaching aide to his friend, Pat Cash. This continued for the next few years as Cash travelled the world, albeit playing more and more as a part-time player. Loccisano continued imparting on Cash many of the messages Barclay had given the 1987 Wimbledon champion for so many years. Loccisano found that his own playing level, plus the education on the game he had received from Barclay over a long period of time, made him at least adequate enough to take on a player still playing at the highest level of the game. He often confided with Barclay on small issues that arose in Cash's game, particularly with regard to technique. Even after the split, typical of Barclay when asked, he couldn't say no to giving assistance.

An Offshore Opportunity

Realising he was available, in late 1991 the British Lawn Tennis Association made an offer to Barclay to take on the position of National Junior Coach, at its Centre of Excellence at Bisham Abbey, situated around 50 kilometres west of London.

Bisham was in general terms the equivalent of the Australian Institute of Sport. Nick Brown urged his mentor to take up the position, knowing firsthand how instrumental he could be to changing around Britain's lagging junior tennis fortunes.

Barclay accepted the opportunity, saying at the time, "I'm disappointed to be leaving Australia, but this is a massive challenge for me." The opportunity would provide him with security in a well-paid job and enable him to keep doing what was closest to his heart, that of developing junior tennis players. Wife Jackie naturally supported his decision.

England had not had a Grand Slam Men's Singles winner since Fred Perry back in 1933 and the country was starved of any real male success.

The British junior tennis development system had for years lacked any real structure or sense of professionalism and as a result, there weren't many bright stars on the horizon. Barclay would be required to work alongside and gain the trust of the country's own coaches while imparting his teachings, ethos and principles to them. Very few coaches had ever attained any ATP points during their playing days. Although not seeing that as essential, the experience therefore would be hard to pass on to any up-and-coming, high-level juniors.

There was the pomp, privacy and closed-door attitudes within some of the private tennis club sector to deal with, as well as a slice of scepticism associated with bringing in someone from outside Britain.

For the lone ranger and visionary in Barclay, the journey ahead would require navigating a few speed humps.

Within the confines of the residential tennis facility were four fast-paced indoor courts, three outdoor clay courts and a gymnasium that included a weightlifting room. One of the first acquaintances Barclay made in his new domain was with his new car. Driving in unfamiliar surrounds frequently saw the often confused coach take wrong turns and end up far from his intended destination.

Barclay's role was to coach the boys in the 12-18 years age bracket at the residential facility, assess the rest of the country's centres for the best talent and make sure that any player invited to the academy had the potential to eventually make it onto the professional tour. Candidates had to be ranked in the top two players in their age group nationally to have any chance of being invited into the academy. Barclay's boss and former tour player, Richard Lewis, asked the new coach to do whatever it took to improve the level of the country's junior tennis stocks. Barclay's inner drive, together with his history of taking young talented tennis players to national and international levels, made him an ideal choice for the role. He knew he could flourish in this new environment. He was ready to start.

Existing UK players still training at the centre included Andrew Foster, Barry Cowan, Miles McClagan, James Baily, Philip Fowler, Lee Sabbin, Mark Schofield, Alex Osterrieth and a young 12-year-old named James Trotman.

Like many new children starting off in the game of tennis, Trotman, as a young six-year-old, had tagged along to the local club with his parents each weekend. Between or after sets, if allowed, he would jump onto the court for a hit with either at the first opportunity. Finding he could hit the ball over the net reasonably well, he enjoyed the experience, kept playing, improved and as he got older eventually went on to win some local tournaments that would include a county junior championship.

Trotman became more well known after winning the national 12 and Under title. On the strength of this win, he was assessed for a position at the academy and offered a position.

Barclay arrived at Bisham Abbey, ready to commence duties. There was a new buzz about the place. Young Trotman's first memories were of each boy having a private lesson with the new coach, which included their strokes being filmed by the video analysis system that Barclay had immediately implemented. He eagerly waited his turn as one by one the boys returned with a summation from their session. Positive responses flooded back from each boy. This was cutting-edge technology for them. They could now see for themselves their own technical strengths and deficiencies.

Ian instructing Simon Dickson

As some of the older boys gradually departed Bisham, other top juniors arrived at the sports centre at different stages.

They included boys like Martin Lee, David Sherwood, Simon Dickson, Lee Childs, Daniel Kiernan, James Auckland, James Nelson, Ben Riby and Jamie Delgado. They all presented different playing abilities and personality traits.

Lee possessed a very competitive streak. Dickson had an incredibly strong work ethic.

Sherwood, although highly talented, had self-discipline issues and had an innate desire to look for trouble and escape from the place at every opportunity. Childs came from a very tight knit family.

Living away from home initially presented issues for Trotman and some of the other boys, but they soon found Barclay taking on not only the tennis coaching role, but together with wife Jackie, the creation of a family environment. Simple things like helping them improve their communication skills, reinforcing proper manners at the dinner table, and respect for others were the pair's daily reminders for all the boys.

Upon beginning the next phase of his tennis journey, Trotman recalled Barclay being the first coach to teach him the correct fundamentals of the game. "I had huge technical deficiencies. My serve was terrible, my forehand had funky things going on with it, and I couldn't volley." Barclay began the long process of taking the young player's game apart and rebuilding it. Like many before him, that again meant hours and hours spent on the practice court.

Thirteen-year-old Lee from Dulwich, London, had started playing tennis as a five-year-old, taught by his tennis coach father. He wasn't pushed, rather allowed to just enjoy the game. Lee was a lover of most sports, particularly football and hockey of which he had played plenty. He followed his beloved Millwall Football Club.

Six months prior to Barclay arriving at Bisham, Lee had trialled for a position, but had been turned down. He quickly caught Barclay's eye around the tennis scene. The young player, ranked three in his age group in the country, was immediately offered a position by the new coach and not long into the New Year joined the squad. He quickly found his feet around the other boys and both Ian and Jackie.

As during his short campaign with the British Davis Cup squad, Barclay began to educate his new young players about the geometry of the tennis court, the art and effectiveness of using angles and depth in the game to their advantage. How to defend and when and how to attack. Tennis for them now took on a more serious element of genuinely learning how to play the game. He wanted them to be able to compete against the best juniors both within and ultimately outside of their homeland.

Trotman, one of the younger boys at the centre, often played in events underage. He acknowledged that time spent on the coaching court with Barclay was tough and hard but there was always an element of fun to go with it. "Barkers would kick our arse one minute then share the funniest joke the next. You would hear him call out from close by or from another court, "Whatever you do, don't hit the net!! Make sure you get your first serve in!! Move your feet!!" Or his favourite one, "Just do it!!" When Barkers said something, it stuck in your head. Many times it was something very simple coated with common sense. It was never questioned. You believed it and just got on with it." Barclay had a certain soft spot for young Trotman. The boy had a twinkle in his eye, and a certain mischievous streak about him. He showed a big heart, which impressed Barclay no end.

Bisham Abbey was an exciting place to both train and reside for these young, enthusiastic tennis players. Bisham was thus the perfect place to live and train.

The English soccer and rugby teams trained there before international games. The Olympic weightlifting team used the gymnasium facilities, as did the rowers. The place was full of elite athletes who trained alongside the tennis players.

Barclay and his band of young players witnessed firsthand how the elite in different sports trained. Lee Childs and James Nelson often leaned out of their windows, conveniently situated behind the abbey, and listened to interviews being conducted with football stars such as Paul Gascoigne.

On The Road Again

Barclay decided the National Junior Squad needed to travel to gain more experience, a decision similar to the one made back in Australia during 1978.

That meant going abroad. They too needed to play on the European clay for exactly the same reasons as the Australian MATCH kids – Cash, Hartnett, the Minter sisters, and others.

Suddenly, 12-year-old Trotman and 13-year-old Martin Lee found themselves playing in some of the strongest 14 and Under tournaments, such as Livorno in Italy and Tarbes in south-west France, which hosted the most prestigious 14 and Under European event of all – the Les Petits As.

Jackie Barclay again went along, still having a good enough grasp of the foreign languages to help with communication issues. Like the Australian juniors in the late 1970s, playing on European clay for the first time was a daunting prospect for the young British players. It took time to adapt.

Early on, Trotman remembered thinking he could win, but came off the court from matches scratching his head in amazement as to how tough it was to win points, let alone games. Barclay needed to use plenty of his experience and guile to help his young team survive. That meant at times dishing out some harsh verbal lessons. The English press often paid out heavily on him. He had already been labelled the son of a wild colonial after once publicly questioning the inner strength of his young British charges.

Ex-Russian female player from the 1970s, Olga Morozova, ran the girls' division at Bisham Abbey. Barclay often lent her his assistance.

He travelled to the ITF junior tournaments when the boys' and girls' teams were both represented and kept an eye on both. The junior girls rarely tasted success, but they provided plenty of life and fun at the centre. They loved to joke around with Barclay often taking the mickey out of him. If he fell asleep in his office chair they would jokingly plait his white mane of hair. During one practice session they dressed him in a tutu and sprayed his hair pink. Some thought him mad for allowing such antics. He knew otherwise. The most important thing to him was to have happy people around the place.

Dean Barclay moved across to London to further develop his own coaching experience. Possessing some of the same inherent coaching qualities as his father, at times they worked closely together. They kept a diary full of the names of juniors that the centre's squad competed against at different tournaments. The diary detailed each opposition player's strengths and weaknesses. Dean also took on some of his own players and sometimes travelled with his father's teams. There was always an Aussie professional playing somewhere around the world if practice partners or some assistance were needed. The younger Barclay then worked for the German Tennis Federation where he lived for two years. He worked alongside highly ranked German male players such as Eric Jelen, Carl Uwe Steeb and Patrick Kuhnen. He also spent time as an assistant coach for the British Federation Cup team.

In 1992, Ian and Jackie relocated to Pinkneys Green, Maidenhead, not far from Bisham, where they lived for the next seven years. Brad Barclay then travelled overseas to spend some time with his parents. He stayed on for two years in London and Europe, much of the time earning money pouring beers in a London hotel.

A year or so into Barclay's tenure at Bisham Abbey, the return for his efforts had shown only meagre results. Having already teamed up with Barclay during the coach's Davis Cup squad duties a couple of years earlier, James Turner decided after numerous knee and other operations that he'd had enough of trying to make endless comebacks onto the tough professional tour. He approached the LTA, keen to try his hand at some coaching. It transpired that at the same time, Barclay was looking for an assistant coach to help him at Bisham Abbey.

On hearing the ex-Davis Cup member had expressed an interest, he quickly spoke up, saying, "I'll take Jimmy." Barclay knew Turner's strong work ethic could translate well into the coaching arena. The new assistant quickly got down to work. He walked around gathering up the endless tennis balls used on the practice courts, whilst soaking up valuable information Barclay passed on to the young squad members.

The coach's discussion could revolve around anything from the important benefit of a small grip change for a stroke, to technically committing to a longer follow through on a stroke during a big point, or to emphasising the importance of winning the first point of every new game. Turner had a tough streak and if any student didn't pay attention to Barclay's instructions he would let them know in no uncertain terms. He desperately wanted the boys to get the same value he had received from his coach two years beforehand.

Turner fell in love with the new opportunity granted him and worked alongside Barclay for the next six years.

While conducting his session, Turner often saw Barclay walk on to a court carrying a heavy bag over each shoulder in order to top dress an area in need of more surface clay. This was a job he had carried out for years on his own home court in Park Orchards and at the Heatherdale Tennis Club. If a chewed-up tennis court needed repairs, Barclay would do it to make sure his squad could maximise their hitting time. This was Barclay going to the nth degree. "Barker's commitment to the cause turned him into a god-like figure to the boys at the centre. They were desperate to prove to him that they could play the game," said Turner.

Barclay brought in another assistant coach, ex-squad junior, Philip Fowler. While attending college in Atlanta, Georgia, Fowler received a surprise call from Barclay, offering him up the chance to come on board. Barely able to believe who was on the other end of the line, Fowler jumped at the opportunity. The northern Englishman had already experienced time with Barclay at Bisham Abbey during the Australian coach's first six months in charge and attributed a strong result in an ITF Grade 2 event to Barclay's both positive and nurturing ways. Although softer in nature, like Turner he too bent over backwards to do anything Barclay asked of him. Barclay quickly had a black notebook in Fowler's hands, having him on the ready to take any relevant notes on students.

The three men formed the coaching panel, their personalities complementing each other. Turner took the boys for morning training before their school day started, Fowler the gym training in the evening, with Barclay overseeing the entire program. The support structure was extensive. A psychologist, sports masseur, physical trainer and physiotherapist were constantly on hand to give treatment to the players and staff. He got great satisfaction from the centre's unique pre-puberty weightlifting program which vastly reduced the potential of injury to his students.

Among the trips abroad to further their development, the squad journeyed to the US to compete on the Florida winter junior circuit which took in the Eddie Herr, the Sunshine Cup, the Continental Cup and the prestigious Orange Bowl tournaments.

While there they stayed, trained and relaxed with Barclay's long-time friend Bob Butterfield at his East Lake Woodlands Tennis Academy.

The two coaches' association had dated back to their Melbourne pennant days, when Barclay played for East Malvern and Butterfield for Royal South Yarra Tennis Clubs. They had shared many experiences playing in the same Australian tennis circles. Butterfield made the decision to head to the US and further his education in the American college system. In the early 1970s, his tennis background was discovered and he was asked by Harry Hopman if he would like to take on a coaching role at Hopman's Port Washington Academy in Long Island, New York. He got to work with a very young John McEnroe and Vitas Gerulaitis. Years on, he set up his own academy in America.

The typical squad training week at Bisham Abbey took in Monday, Tuesday, Wednesday and Friday, which was a combination of tennis and gym work. The weekend was spent travelling around Great Britain or beyond playing tournaments. The surfaces played on were either grass, hard court or clay (a shale type of covering). If a player came back injured or tired, Barclay would give them Monday off.

Barclay knew that in order to toughen up his boys, at times he had to be cruel to be kind. He refused to offer up praise for the sake of it.

It was a matter-of-fact approach that he used, particularly with Lee, in order to get the best out of him.

One night they were all returning to Bisham after playing a three-day tournament.

Ian with members of the LTA Bisham Abbey junior squad – Simon Dickson, Martin Lee, James Trotman and David Sherwood

The four-wheel drive they were in had a sunroof. Barclay conned one of the boys into giving him a runner's up trophy they had received.

Seeing no cars were behind him, he opened the sunroof and threw the trophy out, the boys stunned at seeing their prize smash to bits on the road behind.

Barclay told the group that he didn't accept second place at the centre because no one ever remembers who came runner-up. Their shock eventually turned to laughter at their coach's action. "I'm sure they wanted to kill me for it at the time," he said. "The result was, we had a lot fewer runners-up trophies in future tournaments." Persistence and hard work began to pay off. Martin Lee won the national age 16 and Under championship, aged 15.

After a typically strenuous week at the academy, Barclay often took a few of the kids back home where he and Jackie made sure they got plenty of rest and sleep, so they could return to the centre fresh for the next block of training. Jackie knew Ian had gone to London wholeheartedly determined to improve the level of tennis in the country's juniors.

Success in the Motherland

As part of his tenure, every few weeks Barclay went to a different private county club to look at promising young players competing in under-age tournaments and help the local coach as well as the official county coach. He gave instructions to the coaches to work on certain aspects of each pupil's games. Having access to video analysis, Barclay made it a requirement for those coaches to return recordings of each coaching session, so he could ascertain if they were doing their job. Some were being paid handsomely. Any brushing over of corrections to a student's technique or movement could be detected. In Barclay's words, "The camera never tells any lies." He needed to keep each coach accountable.

Every Monday morning it was a requirement that they all have their tournament reports from across the weekend handed in at the centre for Barclay's perusal, including which children won and who showed promise. The female coaches tied to the girls' section never failed to meet the deadline.

Coaches from various counties often brought their students and squads to Bisham for Barclay to assess and tweak any necessary part of their game. As with his own squad, a substantial amount of time and repetition on court could be needed in order to rectify a problem. The centre had a special video room set aside.

One of Barclay's evolving methods was to ask students to view any changes made and come back to him with an opinion as to whether the change felt comfortable, but more importantly whether they believed the stroke would stand up under extreme pressure. He wanted them to take ownership of their own game. Hence he would then make them play practice sets as a gauge. If the change failed, he would go back again to the practice court to find an answer. Others coming in to the centre also encouraged a healthy rivalry between squads, with the outsiders wanting to take on and beat the Bisham boys. The level of tennis across the board began to improve.

Barclay had James Trotman and one of the centre's girls, Abbey Tordoff, enter the 'Player Plus' tournament, about 100 kms outside London. The event allowed coaches on court to advise players. With a cash prize on offer to both players and coach, Trotman's nerves showed and at one point struggled to hold a cup of water his coach had poured for him at the change of ends. The pair won the tournament. Typically of Barclay, he wasn't interested in any personal financial gain. He wanted the money to go to an underprivileged young person, who could have tennis lessons. A nice letter eventually arrived at the centre from the recipient of the gift, thanking the group. That same player had won their first tournament.

Barclay stayed in touch with Nick Brown. Keeping himself busy, Brown had picked up work with some of the Women's Tennis Association (WTA) tour players such as Russian Elena Likhovtseva and Zimbabwe's Cara Black, both multiple Grand Slam doubles and mixed doubles winners.

Brown's father-in-law was English soccer legend Sir Bobby Charlton. As a charitable gesture, together Barclay and Charlton organised for a number of buses to transport some of Manchester's most underprivileged children to local tennis centres to give them an opportunity to play the game. Naturally Barclay kept a keen eye on any talent that might have emerged.

Barclay and Brown were asked by Brown's friend Victor Archutowski to go to Poland to have a look at two talented young juniors. They arrived to six inches of deep snow in the town of Lodz (pronounced Wootch). Their hospitable Polish hosts welcomed both men in the customary way, which was by drinking a glass of vodka, which Barclay said "tasted like rocket fuel". They were then taken on a tour of the local village. The father, a doctor, was very keen on tennis. Over dinner, Barclay as usual, told tennis stories. The night eventuated into a test of both coach and doctor trying to drink each other under the table with the local brew. Somehow Brown recalled his mentor managed to survive the night, albeit waking the next morning feeling very poorly.

The academy boys practised plenty of doubles. Learning to play doubles correctly had been the Barclay way for years. There was stringent attention paid to practice on first serve placement, return of serve, making the first volley down the middle of the court, crossing on the biggest points of the match and other subtle nuances of the game. The hours spent labouring away at doubles drills became second nature and they eventually realised what was required to play the game well. The winter weather made it impossible to practice outside, so the indoor courts saw plenty of doubles played. Every week, wherever they were in the world, it was mandatory to practice their doubles skills. This was Barclay going to the nth degree.

The Rover Initiative Scheme was put in place by the LTA's marketing man, Paul Hutchins. Chief sponsor of the Centre of Excellence, the Rover Car Company, injected the necessary funds into the tennis program that allowed Barclay and his team to spread their wings.

Examples of its advertising deals were seen on the facility's walls where billboards were hung. Barclay was given a new car annually.

Each player wore the sponsor's patch on all their tennis shirts, which Jackie religiously sewed on before each tournament

Aged 16, Martin Lee made the final of the national 18 and Under Singles championships.

1995 proved a breakthrough year. Barclay had given Simon Dickson the nickname 'Rocky'. Having come from an extremely modest background, he didn't want for much, but was prepared to give everything of himself, both on the practice court and in matches.

Ian with James Trotman and Martin Lee sporting the Rover logo in front of the sponsor's car

Dickson and his Great Britain team captured both the 14 and Under World Junior Team Championships in Japan and the European Team Championships (Copa del Sol) in Spain.

Dickson and James Trotman both won European Junior Championship Doubles titles in different age groups. Martin Lee made the singles final at both the Italian Open Juniors and the Astrid Bowl Belgium International.

Barclay's boys then had a major triumph. James Trotman and Martin Lee won the Wimbledon Boys' Doubles, defeating Mexican Alejandro Hernandez and Argentine Mariano Puerto 7-6, 6-4.

In the dressing room before the boys Wimbledon final, a somewhat nervous Trotman asked Barclay how many spectators were sitting in the stands. To help ease his nerves Barclay replied he could only count about seven.

On entering the court, the British boys were confronted with what appeared to be more like 7000. Trotman quietly swore at his coach who was sitting in readiness close to the entrance.

1995 Junior Wimbledon Doubles Champions
Martin Lee and James Trotman

The rare British feat had brought a packed house to the junior final. When Trotman crossed and put away the winning volley on match point, the crowd went wild.

The final was played on Court One, adjacent to the centre court where Boris Becker was playing Pete Sampras in the Men's Singles final.

On hearing the commotion nearby, Becker went up to the central umpire and flippantly enquired as to how it was possible that a bigger match was happening at the same time as the one he and Sampras were playing.

"The wonderful straight sets 7-6 (2) 6-4 victory to these British boys gave everybody in the system such a huge boost. Not in their wildest dreams could they have imagined standing in front of royalty to accept the winning cup," said Barclay.

The Australian coach had gone a long way towards helping change his adopted country's tennis identity and culture. There was a disease that hadn't caught on in British junior tennis like it had elsewhere around the world. It was called the 'winning' disease.

Finally this new stream reared its head, spread, and became far more prominent than the losing syndrome they had known for so long.

When one boy won something of significance, the whole psychic changed. They went from being bottom of the pile to suddenly winning tournaments.

Ironically, the newspaper tabloids left Barclay alone and centred their energy on the great exploits of the country's new tennis heroes, the first British juniors to win a Wimbledon Junior Boys' Final. James Trotman then won the national 18 and Under title, aged 16.

Martin Lee, aged 17, made yet another singles final at the end of the year, at the Eddie Herr International in the US. It took him to an unprecedented number three singles ranking in the ITF 18 and Under age group.

Simon Dickson won the 14 and Under at Eddie Herr and then reached the final of the 14 and Under Orange Bowl Singles.

Ian talking tactics with 1996 world number one junior Martin Lee during the Sunshine Cup, held in Fort Lauderdale, Florida

The thought of top ten world rankings for his academy boys was motivation enough for Barclay to drive them on further.

Ironically, while practising at Rick Macci's Tennis Academy in Boca Raton, Florida, Richard Williams, father of Americans Venus and Serena, happened to stroll past Barclay squad. He yelled out to Barclay, "Hey, old man, keep hitting those balls back. One day you may make it to Wimbledon. Barclay saw the funny side.

During a rare break, Barclay took the opportunity to play in an Over 55s event in Singapore. Aged 57, he asked the squad to train him in the indoor centre. He made them turn the heating up so to simulate the conditions he would be facing again in the hot Far East. The boys ran him ragged, frequently yelling out, "Come on, run, you old bugger." He was fit, but had to be in top condition for the upcoming tournament. He made the final with wife Jackie watching the match. The heat had been so intense throughout the week that he literally staggered to the baseline to serve on match point. She had seen some warning signs earlier in the match and had wanted him to stop playing. Only a year earlier a family friend had died from a massive heart attack playing in the same tournament.

Whenever Barclay looked up into the crowd, the 300 or so people there watching looked more like thousands to him. This time it wasn't the Barclay exaggeration. Post-match after finally winning, he couldn't help himself. "I organised a party for everyone and spent all the prize money on booze. Jackie never forgave me."

Barclay's ex-assistant coach from Heatherdale Tennis Club, Martin Kozma decided to further his own coaching career as well, leaving Australia to live and work overseas. He linked up with Jackie and Ian at their Pinkneys Green house. Over the next five years, Kozma lived and worked closely with Barclay, also helping out with his juniors and others with whom he was connected. Kozma saw that nothing had fundamentally changed in the way Barclay coached his young male British players, compared to when he was back at Heatherdale during the 1970s. Now he was more worldly and switched on to the needs of the next generation of players.

UK Success Down Under and Beyond

The fruits of Barclay's labour then bore more striking results. In 1996, for a second consecutive year, he brought his British juniors down to Australia for the summer season. Starting in early January at the Victorian regional town of Traralgon for the ITF Grade 2 event, Martin Lee won the Boys' Singles. A singles semi-final showing by Lee at the Australian Junior Hardcourts Grade 1 event at the Notting Hill Pinewood Tennis Club then saw he and James Trotman reach the final of the Australian Open Boys' Doubles.

James Trotman proceeded to make the final of the Grade 1 Japan Open Boys' Singles. He and Lee won the Doubles title and in May, the boys captured the Italian Open Boys' Doubles title to now confirm their ranking as number one and two junior doubles players in the world.

Martin Lee continued to have strong singles results. He reached the final of the Roehampton Grade 1 Boys' Singles and won the Yucatan Cup Boys' Singles at the end of the year. During the year, Lee, aged 18, officially took over the number one world junior singles ranking, at the same time holding the number one doubles ranking.

Barclay had proved to himself and others that a British boy could reach the pinnacle of world junior tennis.

Time, patience, learning how to play the game, working harder, getting better, and dealing with the pressure of expectation had all been elements that Lee and his other squad members had faced under Barclay's guidance. He felt the system had now been rewarded. With the pressure to perform, however, came the inevitable added scrutiny of the British media. During tournaments Barclay simply reminded Lee that he was the best junior in the world and to play like he owned the position, a strategy he'd used with Pat Cash a decade earlier. Lee then made his ATP senior debut at the Queen's Club tournament, which preceded Wimbledon.

In 1997, the Bisham boys again held centre stage, this time Down Under.

James Trotman and David Sherwood defeated South Africans Jaco van der Westhuizen and Wesley Whitehouse 7-6, 6-3, to win the Australian Open Boys' Doubles title.

Delighted, Barclay showed again it was possible to win back on home soil with a team from the other side of the world.

Sherwood continued to feature strongly in doubles as the year unfolded, making the final of the World Super Junior Championships in Japan with Simon Dickson in October.

Yet again in 1998 Barclay brought his UK junior team down to Australia for another summer season, thus making it his fourth consecutive trip.

Simon Dickson and David Sherwood, who had won the Eddie Herr Boys' Doubles in the US, won both the ITF Doubles events at Traralgon and Notting Hill Pinewood, and Sherwood reached the singles semi-final at Traralgon.

Ian with James Trotman and David Sherwood at Melbourne Park

With Lee Childs reaching a final the following year at Traralgon, it gave Barclay a total of six finals appearances, including a Grand Slam title, at international level back in his home country. One might suggest that with those numbers, combined with the development of junior tennis in the UK under his watch, the decision by Tennis Australia not to offer him a coaching position nine years earlier had somewhat come back to bite it.

In the years he had been at Bisham Abbey, albeit with a few exceptions, he had turned around the largely underperforming country's junior tennis fortunes. Had he been afforded a similar role back in his home country, it may well have seen Australia's own junior tennis reach greater heights.

Barclay worked all the Bisham boys extremely hard, often telling them if they had to go onto the tennis court on crutches to play, then so be it. It was one of his methods to help toughen them up. "I had to be hard on the boys because we had a few softies during the early days and we were so far behind the rest of the world. When I arrived in England, I believed their tennis was two and a half to three years behind the Australian kids and it was the year 1991."

He admits both Martin Lee and James Trotman often played with injuries. "During one tournament in France, Trotters, who was tough by nature, played with two stress fractures in his feet. I had to cut his shoes from his feet and put both in ice, his feet were that swollen." He doesn't shy away from taking ownership for some of the repetitive injuries to his young charges, such as wrist problems, tennis elbow and shin splints. "It was my fault. At times I worked them too hard, there's no doubt about that. I found myself conflicted, both being in a hurry to produce good players, but at the same time needing to demonstrate patience, due in part to their immaturity on a world scale. The boys themselves didn't want days off. They felt any time off could see them fall behind.

"We played on different surfaces and they wore a variety of shoes. At times I looked for methods by which I could lessen the work rate. For example, if a boy made a final of a tournament on a Sunday, I would give them Monday off and then give them all Thursday off, so they could have a rub-down and a swim."

Often maligned for their perceived lack of toughness, Barclay's methods proved their worth. Assistant James Turner took Martin Lee to Manilla in the Philippines for a Grade 2 ITF junior event, where he had to contend with several matches that included both singles and doubles finals on the one day in sweltering heat.

Turner, watching from the stands, was unimpressed with a couple of sloppy shots played by the academy's top player. Set to berate the player post match, as Lee walked off the court, he proceeded to throw up all over himself, having suffered from the effects of heat exhaustion. His opponent fared worse, taken to a local hospital and placed on a drip. Turner also took academy boys to the harsh environs of South America, where again they played against some of the strongest clay court juniors in the world, often playing through illness and injury to record solid results. Barclay's ethos of hard work reflected strongly in his boys. Whatever it took to get through matches, they did it.

Barclay attributed much of the success to his assistants, Turner and Fowler. "The boys were just so keen and they constantly wanted to learn and improve their coaching skills and help all the boys at the centre improve their tennis. I was also hard on Jimmy and Phil, at times asking them to do the near impossible. The hours they put in were extraordinary."

James Trotman eventually succumbed to his injuries, which for Barclay was a great disappointment. Like protégé Mark Hartnett years earlier, his body could no longer hold up, therefore in Barclay's mind cutting short yet another potentially fine tennis career.

Albeit, Trotman attributed his success entirely to his education from his Australian coach. He believed he played his best level of junior doubles towards the end of his junior career, solely based on the hundreds of hours spent on court honing those skills. There were plenty of difficult days on court but in Trotman's words, "The work we did was enormous, it was never easy, but I think we got there in the end."

Eye for Talent

Barclay's influence reached farther out than the Bisham Abbey walls.

Victor Archutowski called and told the coach that he had organised to bring a young teenage girl out from Belarus and could he have a look at her game. Olga Barabanschikova was a very talented player and showed plenty of promise. Barclay's son Dean and Kozma both came on board at different times to assist in her journey. Claiming three ITF Junior Singles titles, she also won the 1996 Wimbledon Junior Girls' doubles with French girl Amelie Mauresmo, then turned professional while still a teenager and ultimately reached a career-high singles ranking of 49 in 1998.

Barclay was at a tournament in Moenchengladbach, Germany, that had a 12 and Under age event. One of the representatives from IMG approached him and wanted his opinion. Of the 128 boys and girls at the tournament, who amongst all in the coach's view stood out in the field and would he like to take on if the opportunity arose? After close examination Barclay noted a tall, young, very athletic Hungarian girl. Her name was Reka Vidats. Barclay said to the agent he thought she showed some very good signs.

Word got back to the young girl's parents, who had both been high-achieving athletes in Hungary. They contacted Barclay and one thing led another. Before he knew it Barclay was on his way to the Hungarian capital, Budapest.

His artistic eye caught sight of a number of beautiful museums and architecture in the main city. He began coaching Vidats, who at times stayed in London with Ian and Jackie and trained with the Bisham Abbey squad. Dean Barclay also took on a coaching role with the young Hungarian, alongside his father. She played at the Bisham boys' level of tennis and brought the best out in the coach's players. Barclay was impressed at how well organised she was with both her personal and professional life. He felt she had a similar strong work ethic to his one-time Australian protégé Anne Minter. Barclay believed she could easily have reached a top ten world ranking.

Barclay was able to get Vidats a substantial contract with sports company Ellesse. However, overnight, the landscape dramatically changed for Ian and Dean. Both coaches suddenly no longer had any further contact with the young protégé, taken out of the picture.

Although disappointed by the situation, it reinforced to Barclay the sometimes fickle and cut-throat nature of his sport. Not blaming the young girl, he ran into her years later in London. She had given the sport away. The promising young girl, who in the space of three years had results including two European Junior Championships, in 1993 and 1995 and a first-round win over future multi Grand Slam Singles titleholder Martina Hingis, at the 1994 Italian Open Juniors. Barclay pondered what might have been.

Nick Brown came to Barclay eager to put his hat in the ring to help the LTA's junior development cause. More tournaments began popping up around the country and more coaches were put into help develop and nurture clubs.

The die was cast for young scholarship holder Lee Childs at his new home at Bisham Abbey. He took to the centre like a duck to water, not suffering any homesickness. Like all the boys, he attended the local school and on the first day when given a stern testing, he took care of the school bully. He came from Somerset in the south west of England where the weather demanded indoor tennis courts, particularly through the winter. Childs went from practising three or four hours a week and playing weekend tournaments, to a gruelling four hours a day with the fitness component added on. Childs revelled in the hard work and in particular the family environment that Ian and Jackie helped provide. "Barkers just knew how to get each of us going. He was just so natural, quickly got on your wave length and knew what made each of us tick. I loved the practice sessions and listened to his every word."

Childs' improvement was significant. Within a couple of years he won national junior singles titles in both the Under 16 and Under 18 age groups. He also travelled, and in 1998, accompanied by Barclay's son Dean, won the ITF Argentina Junior Hard Court Singles title. Childs was strongly built and it reflected in his game. In Barclay's words, "Lee developed the biggest serve and forehand drive one could imagine. I told him to believe in himself, trust what he had and the results would come. He served so many aces."

Down Time

Among many long-time tennis friends that visited Ian and Jackie, South Australians Jan and Ian MacDonald stayed while on holidays. The local Brown Abbott pub was located just around the corner. Inevitably guests would often find themselves at the hotel for a quenching ale, dinner and the light entertainment on offer. Many a late night was ensured. One night, Ian MacDonald needed a stray supermarket shopping trolley to help wheel home some of the holidaymakers who had overindulged in the local product.

The Bisham Abbey sports centre had a picturesque nine-hole golf course where the coach and his squad sometimes played during their downtime. Barclay had played a bit of golf back in his early Melbourne pennant days, but apart from occasionally playing with Nick Brown or with other visiting friends, he didn't get much time to play. During the evenings, after training, while it was still light, the group sometimes practised chipping and putting and played competitive games.

When time allowed, they played nine holes. "The boys used to cheat like crazy. Trotters always wore a pair of shorts with a hole in one pocket. Every time his ball got stuck under a tree or bush, he would have a spare ready to drop from his pocket in a better position. They conned me left, right and centre and tried every trick in the book to get back at me."

Playing golf was often a timely distraction from the tennis court where Barclay could better get some of his tennis-related messages across to his chargers, with their minds more at ease and receptive.

Barclay eventually joined a golf club, not far from Heathrow Airport and played there sometimes during time off. Barclay and Brown occasionally took to the golf course together. During one particular round, Barclay got off to a solid start, parring the first two holes, before his game started to unravel. As they reached the seventh hole, Barclay, eager to clean his ball, went to the ball washer alongside the tee. He put his ball inside the device and began turning the handle, only to find the ball wouldn't reappear. It was lost. Continuing to turn the handle, there was still no sight of the golf ball, only Brown lying on the ground in hysterics, asking his friend how he was going to explain what had just happened. The loss reflected the remainder of his round, but typically he saw the funny side and it became yet another story at dinner parties and hotel bars around the tennis world.

Ian with great friend and English footballer, David Ford, who played 260 games with Sheffield Wednesday, Newcastle United, Sheffield United and Halifax Town

When the opportunity arose Ian and Jackie went with friends, ex-English footballer David Ford and fellow Aussie tennis coach Bob Butterfield and their wives Angela and Carolyn to various parts of the world for holidays and get-togethers.

On the first of what became an annual holiday trip to Scotland, Barclay and Ford greeted the Butterfields at Manchester Airport, dressed up in full kilt, sporran and all, causing a scene around the arrival gate.

Off the same plane came the Australian Rugby team who were being greeted by hordes of cameramen. The two dressed-up Scots made the evening news.

After picking up their friends, they proceeded to drive back to the Fords' home in Sheffield. Running low on petrol, they stopped at a service station on the way. Barclay and Ford fuelled the tank, then went inside to pay. The attendant immediately put his hands in the air, thinking the two costume-wearing friends were going to rob him.

Golf was usually part of the schedule of events on these sojourns. Said Butterfield, "One favourite memory is playing the St Andrews Old Course, walking down the 18th hole with our wives following, and Ian shanking a shot that hit the roof of the Tommy Morris shop and then bounced back on to the 18th green to the applause of the onlookers. Barkers took a bow and proceeded to miss the putt."

They also played golf in the far north of the country at Royal Dornach, where the wind often played havoc. On one occasion, the women dropped their husbands off at the golf course before travelling to Tamar, a town famous for manufacturing Scottish knitwear, to purchase gifts for their families.

That day, the golfers stopped playing golf only two holes into the round as the wind was so strong, it made playing virtually impossible. The golf balls wouldn't remain still on the greens. So to kill time they headed to the clubhouse bar, where the club members insisted they try some of the local malt whiskey. Barclay had never drunk whiskey in his life. "We were well and truly sucked in. We had promised to take the girls out to dinner that night, but on their return, we were so out of sorts we could barely stand up, let alone escort them anywhere. They didn't forgive us too kindly."

At the end of the 1997 year, on another trip to the US, Bob Butterfield and friends visited Barclay while his squad were in Sarasota, Florida. They had bought him a gift, a zimmer frame decorated with a horn and other accessories to celebrate his 60th birthday. As a surprise, they burst into his hotel room, singing loudly, ringing the horn, ready to open the champagne in celebration. Little did they realise he had only turned 59.

Dark Clouds

Ian Barclay had been at Bisham Abbey for nine years. Members of the junior squad had competed and won titles around the world and at various stages held every national age group title in the country.

Barclay doesn't shy away from the fact that he made enemies along the way in his coaching role in the UK. He had to deal with some harsh private club snobbery.

In the mid 1990s some clubs still didn't allow children to play tennis on their courts. He made a strong suggestion to his boss that unless all the clubs had a coach, a convenor and their juniors playing organised competition, a law should be adopted that each of the clubs' presidents should cease to get their free allocation of yearly Wimbledon tickets. Barclay felt if any real development was to be made in junior tennis, some hard decisions had to be made on its behalf.

Overnight, though, for Ian and Jackie things turned upside down. Administration structures within the LTA began to change. Many of the staff who had worked both behind the scenes and closely alongside Barclay suddenly received huge promotions and equally big wage rises. People with sound business acumen, but very little idea about junior tennis, were being brought in as replacements for some of the old guard.

In a scenario reminiscent of the landscape within Tennis Australia's hierarchy, the new administration running tennis in Britain was now looking like a 'jobs for the boys' affair. This made Barclay both cautious and uncomfortable.

Such was the changing landscape, Barclay was then astonishingly instructed to cease work with any of the junior squad once they reached 18 years of age. He had a gagging order placed on him, which prevented him from talking about the LTA's restructure.

Gradually the tabloids started to question why very few of these highly ranked juniors were progressing. Surely Barclay's record of having a top three world-ranked British junior boy for six consecutive years stood for something? Surely the distinction of having his players winning every national title while he was at the helm stood for something? Obviously not.

It is easy to suggest that like so many years beforehand, jealousy of Barclay's success in developing junior tennis players had reared its ugly head again. Even after offering to help those in charge with coaching his ex-juniors, in an amazing twist of fate Barclay was accused of being unapproachable. The doors now were firmly closed on him. Barclay decided it was best for him and Jackie to leave.

Lee Childs was sorely affected by his coach's exit from Bisham. He was adamant that he wanted to have Barclay's continued help alongside him through that period to help his game. He felt that around his age, to be chopping and changing coaches was more of a detriment to any player's game. His biggest disappointment during the upheaval was that nobody asked the players for their input. "It was like the establishment said this is what's going to happen, end of story, and this is where you are going now. To be honest, at the time it was criminal and still sits uncomfortably inside me even today, all these years later. I just absolutely loved my time at the academy. Given the opportunity, Barkers would fight for us boys all the way." Barclay himself felt much sadness for Childs, who had a particularly close relationship with the coach. He knew his strong, big-serving pupil was ready to take the next step.

When Bisham Abbey closed its doors and with Barclay gone, the young players were farmed out to various centres around the country. Some disenchanted players gradually left the game.

Childs had been at the centre for three and a half years and had put together some strong performances. At 17 years of age, he was sent to the Queen's Club along with James Nelson, Simon Dickson and Ben Riby to train with a newly formed LTA intermediate squad. He no longer had contact with his coach. Toni-Ann Barclay sometimes received telephone calls from Childs initially still upset with his new-found sudden situation. She took Childs across to her father for a few secret hits.

After Barclay's departure, Nick Brown saw the landscape of junior tennis quickly deteriorate. The level of professionalism in all areas of junior development simply dropped off. "It was a very, very sad day when Barkers decided to go back to Australia," said Brown. He and Jackie touched not only mine, but so many other people's lives in the United Kingdom."

James Turner reflected, "The kids were lost, the aftercare wasn't there anymore and they had to literally fend for themselves." It hit home to Turner just how sorely missed Barclay was going to be. Turner doesn't deny that Barclay had his struggles with the establishment. "They tried to close Bisham Abbey down a couple of times while he was there. The fact that Barkers even came in to take on the job from the outset got people's noses out of joint and heightened jealousies among some. The irony was that once those internal figures realised Barclay was in it purely for the kids, it started to change their perspective of him."

Phil Fowler felt the LTA had failed to genuinely recognise Barclay for his efforts in developing its country's junior tennis. "The egos within couldn't come to terms with that nor with his results and success that followed." Fowler knew that Barclay, Turner and himself – the three coaches who made up the coaching panel – weren't necessarily cut from the same cloth as some of the other establishment coaches. They had found a winning formula and were intent on pressing on in their pursuit of development at all costs.

Castle had realised early on that he was working with a coach determined to grow the person, not just the tennis player. This quality of person, he felt, had been sadly lacking in the British tennis establishment for years.

"Ian Barclay was the biggest loss we ever suffered in British tennis," said Andrew Castle. "He was there to help us and we got rid of him. Importantly, Ian was first and foremost a human being. He recognised the frailties and mistakes made by young professional tennis players in their lives along their journey and his strength was in his mentoring. He was about doing the work you needed to do in order to achieve what you wanted to achieve. Being technically perfect as not to break down in critical situations. I don't think anyone ever taught a serve better than Ian. Whenever I went around to Barker's London house, I always felt he thought he was pushing shit uphill with what went on around him. The centre's kids were doing so well but he was always being hounded at the same time. There were always petty jealousies of him. He obviously annoyed the wrong people."

Martin Lee, the player whom arguably achieved the best results of all boys during Barclay's reign, echoed the widespread sentiment felt amongst those closely associated with their coach. "The simple black and white fact was that Barkers had produced both great players and great results, not previously seen in the UK."

Lee had lived at Bisham Abbey for five and a half years. "I found it great fun to live and train at the same facility. Quite a few of the other lads there I had known for years. When we finished our work for the day we could all relax together. I really enjoyed my time there and Barkers made the training enjoyable. Quite often you would laugh so much that you didn't notice how long you had been working for."

Barclay believed the Bisham experience was responsible for Lee's mature outlook. "It was great for Martin. He was the most senior of the boys and had been the most successful. Out of all the boys, he became the one to ring me up to know what the following day's training program would be. There is nothing for building up self-confidence like having a group of people around you who look up to you and admire you. Martin grew up, became a professional player in his own right who could make his own decisions."

Barclay was guardedly optimistic about his charges' prospects of success at the highest level. "The juniors who do come through and have success do so at different stages to each other.

"Swede Thomas Enqvist was a great junior, then achieved nothing for three years. He went on to become top ten on the main tour." Some of his contemporaries in juniors had reached top 50 and Barclay thought Lee would sooner or later join them. Much of Lee's inspiration was drawn from what the country's two best men's players at the time, Tim Henman and Greg Rusedski, were achieving on the tour. Lee initially settled in fairly well on the professional tour, although he found it hard going trying to qualify for tournaments, constantly playing players ranked higher than him in his endeavour to pick up all-important ranking points.

Lee endured the rigours of the professional tour and recorded his best singles result at the Hall of Fame Championships in Newport, Rhode Island in 2001 where he reached the final. He reached the second round at Wimbledon four times and played Davis Cup for his country. Lee recorded a career-high singles ranking of 94 in 2002, to sit only behind Henman and Rusedski as top British-ranked players. His foundation had been laid at Bisham Abbey under Ian.

Ironically Lee Childs, at the end of Bisham Abbey, was on the cusp of much bigger things. During the 2000 year, the strongly built Childs went on to win the European Junior Championship 18 and Under Singles and Doubles in Klosters, Switzerland as well as the US Open Boys' Doubles with James Nelson. He and Nelson finished the year ranked number one junior doubles pair in the world. He also became the youngest player, still under the age of 18, to win his country's Senior National Men's Singles title at Telford. He won the same event again the following year. Lee Childs eventually made it onto the Davis Cup team, as did David Sherwood. Childs played main draw singles, doubles and mixed doubles at Wimbledon for several years, having a win over highly ranked Russian Nikolay Davydenko in five sets in 2003. He won a few Futures events and ultimately reached a singles ranking of around 251 on the ATP tour in 2004.

Back to Oz

After leaving London in 2000, Ian and Jackie Barclay returned to Australia.

Jackie's health had begun to deteriorate late into their UK stay. Barclay's new role in life now extended to that of tennis coach, cook and general housekeeper. It wasn't long before extra assistance for both was offered from family and friends, in particular Jackie's sister, Kay.

The coach had initially returned to Australia, not aligning himself to any tennis club or organisation.

Word quickly spread though that he was back in Melbourne. It wasn't long before the telephone rang and he began conducting lessons again on his Park Orchards backyard court. On the family flip side, Toni-Ann Barclay met English boyfriend Tom Lane and stayed on in London.

Towards the end of his time at Bisham Abbey, Barclay made sure some of his old Melbourne tennis mates put his name down on the prestigious Commonwealth Golf Club's waiting list, having more keenly taken to the sport. He joined the beautiful sand belt course soon after arriving home. It gave him an opportunity to reacquaint, socialise and play with three of his closest old tennis friends, Will Coghlan, Bill Beischer and Barry Brennan, sometimes twice a week.

One day, while having his morning shave, Barclay noticed a lump in his neck. With some pushing, prodding and cutting, a small piece of glass emerged from his skin. Astonishingly, it had been there for around 40 years, never removed through surgery from the injury he had suffered in the car accident with Ray O'Connor decades earlier. It remains a souvenir.

A chance meeting in the summer of 2001 with a former state junior team representative proved timely for Barclay. During the summer school holiday junior tournament period, Steve Wood had his 12-year-old son, Ryan, playing at the outer eastern suburban Ringwood Tennis Club. He looked up and spotted the familiar figure with the same striking mane of white hair he had previously known, heading his way. It was Barclay.

Wood's memory momentarily took him back to the time he faced a young Patrick Cash at the Glen Iris junior tournament in the final of the Under 15 Boys' Singles many years earlier. A three-set defeat at the hands of the younger Cash was the first of five consecutive losses for Wood who remembered two things. Each consecutive loss got worse and he always felt that not only was he playing against a real talent, but against his foe's coach as well, who as always sat courtside during Cash's matches.

In the late 1970s, Wood, for a period of time, held the number one junior ranking in Victoria. He had formed a part of the state's Linton Cup team, which competed in New South Wales under Barclay's guidance. In the team environment, Barclay was thankfully in his corner and he relished the opportunity to be around the coach, who he thought operated at a far different level of professionalism than he had ever been used to previously.

Wood then lost contact with Barclay for a number of years. Post his junior days, he went on to Louisiana State University in America, then played on the professional tennis circuit for a couple of years before becoming involved in the technology industry. He had built up 18 years of business experience as chief executive of information, communication and technology companies in Australia, across the Asia-Pacific region and around the world. "In that time, Barkers had taken Pat through to the semi-finals of the US Open which I remember watching live from my home in the States. This was followed by his coup de grace at Wimbledon. It was just wonderful to see him deliver a world champion. Watching them at the time, I really felt they were both Australian sporting heroes. Knowing Barkers had taken Pat from grassroots tennis to a Grand Slam title, end to end, showed he was one of the very few coaches in the world to achieve such a feat. To also think that at one time in my life I had played both with and against a future Wimbledon champion was a special feeling."

On reacquainting, Wood jokingly reminded Barclay how famous he was through his exploits with Cash and the distinctive head of white hair that had seen its fair share of television coverage over the years. Wood then asked Barclay if he could teach his son how to hit a better forehand. "No trouble," was the coach's answer, only too happy to help out.

It hadn't taken long, but now his weekly diary of tennis lessons had become full.

Other Talents

A young boy had arrived on Barclay's Park Orchards doorstep from Sydney. He was an 11-year-old called Andrew Thomas, of Greek Cypriot origin. Barclay had first seen the young player in the Harbour City when the boy's parents asked the coach for his assessment of their son, then 10 years old. His tennis greatly impressed Barclay, but like many, needed plenty of time spent on his game. "He had this amazing eye. Technically he wasn't much chop, but he had an incredible eye for the game," was the coach's verdict of Thomas.

Like Bernadette Randall years earlier, Thomas' parents brought their son down to Melbourne from the northern state with the intent of having coaching from Barclay. He said yes but added it was a hell of a long way to come from Sydney. The next thing the coach knew, the family had sold their business and home and had moved in just around the corner from Barclay's home.

Barclay began the technical makeover of his new young pupil, as well as the development of a more all court game. The young boy's hero was the great American, 14-time Grand Slam Singles winner, Pete Sampras. Like others before him, Thomas improved rapidly under his new coach. He began to lift junior trophies in his own age group around Victoria. Like Mark Hartnett and Pat Cash years beforehand, he started to win outside his age as well. Barclay believed the young Sydney boy had some serious talent.

Not long after their chance meeting at the Ringwood Tennis Club, Steve Wood received a telephone call from Barclay. The coach's first words were, "Steve, I think I've got another one." Wood asked him what he meant. Barclay replied, "I think I've got another Pat Cash." Replied Wood, "But, Barkers, you've always got players coming through that tennis factory of yours. Why is this one so special?"

The coach explained that he thought like both Cash and Hartnett at a similar age, the boy was a rare talent whose rhythm and timing on his strokes were a cut above the rest. At times it left him dumbfounded. Barclay told Wood that 22 years on, yet again, in order to see some of the new talent realised, he needed to put together another financial syndicate to help with future expenses.

Wood told Barclay he thought he might be able to help pull the project together. Wood contacted a familiar name in Richard Neville-Smith, who had invested in the MATCH project back in 1979. Both Wood and Neville Smith subsequently took on the sponsorship of the new prodigy. With their assistance, Barclay could take Andrew Thomas and his tennis further afar.

The year 2002 proved a big year. Andrew Thomas' development continued, with wins early in the year at both the Tasmania and Canberra national junior titles, followed up by a runner-up result in the national grass court 12 and Under championships.

Steve Wood and his family then accompanied Barclay, wife Jackie and young Thomas on an overseas trip back to the UK, which included taking in a visit to Wimbledon. While visiting Scotland, the young 12-year-old played in the national 14 and Under championships finishing runner-up, along the way defeating players at least two years older.

Ian and Jackie took the opportunity to catch up with many of their long-standing friends. It didn't take long to find a local hotel, where generally several Pimms were devoured along with much reminiscing.

In September, Andrew Thomas won the 12 and Under national junior title at Melbourne Park, taking the final in a remarkable 23 minutes without dropping a game. Barclay thought one of two things had happened. Either the young boy possessed exceptional talent, or the rest of the juniors in his year were not up to the mark.

He suggested to those in the syndicate that he would like to take the young player to the Orange Bowl in Miami, Florida in December to find out how good he really was. He proceeded to destroy all opponents, winning the 12 and Under event in Miami, his final three matches with the loss of only 10 games. It staggered Barclay. He had forced himself not to get carried away after the home national title win. "I thought it might end up a bad year. I was wrong. When you do what he did at the Orange Bowl, it can only give you hope. The way I look at it, while he was so young and there was such a long way to go, at least it's better to have somebody that's got enormous talent than somebody you just hope you will pluck out of the sky." Barclay thought he hadn't seen a 12-year-old anywhere like Thomas.

Ann Quinn, long-time Barclay accomplice and fitness advisor to Barclay's greatest success, Pat Cash was recruited to help out.

Barclay realised he needed to develop Thomas' serve and forehand into stronger weapons. Without these, the coach conceded no player had a chance of succeeding at the highest level in the modern game. Thomas went on a modified school program in order to spend more time on the practice court. Recognising the risks of injury and burnout, holding the young charge back was one of Barclay's biggest challenges. "Half the time I said to myself I should be taking it easier with Andrew and give him more blocks of time off, but he was just so keen. It was difficult, but like with my Bisham Abbey academy boys, I forced him onwards."

In 2003, Steve Wood's father and brother were in New York for the US Open. Wood had amassed plenty of Frequent Flyer points through his work flying across the Asia Pacific region. He offered Barclay a boys' weekend away in New York to help use up some of the points, give the coach some time away from the tennis court, as well as catch up with some of his own family living abroad. They had four days in the Big Apple, most of it ironically spent walking around the famous Flushing Meadow tennis centre. Barclay couldn't help himself, constantly searching, looking for players with the biggest and best games.

They still found time to shop, buy presents for family, hang out over a couple of Budweiser beers, get upgraded to first class on the return flight to Melbourne and reminisce over a great four days back on the other side on the world.

Wood put it to Barclay that he had watched so much junior tennis that the two men should get together and play some doubles. They teamed up to play in the 2003 ITF Victorian Hardcourt 45 Years and Over Seniors' event at Kooyong. Barclay was 68 years young. They won the event, Wood remarking laughingly, "It's the only time I ever played on the same side of the net as him."

In January of 2004, Andrew Thomas won the world-renowned European 14 and Under junior tournament, Les Petits As.

Yet again, however, just at the wrong time, an unexpected turn of events happened in Barclay's life. Having progressed so well up to this point, the young boy suddenly encountered a family upheaval in the form of a parent separation, which in turn changed the course of his own life.

With barely a word said, Barclay saw his Orange Bowl and European winner relocate back to Sydney, virtually overnight. He and his highly talented junior were suddenly apart, out of touch. Barclay felt empty.

Never too far from Barclay's mind, however, were his other sporting loves of football, golf and horse racing. If the tennis scene threw up a difficult challenge, he could quite easily take time out and indulge in any of these interests.

Although Thomas ultimately stayed in the game and played on the world's lower-level futures and challenger circuits for a time, deep down Barclay sadly felt a great opportunity and potential career may have been lost. "Andrew Thomas as a junior was in another class, he was that good," said Barclay. "But sadly he is yet another example where for any one of a myriad of reasons, great young players can get lost along the way."

Out on his backyard court in Park Orchards, Barclay found yet another prospect, Melbourne boy, Will Heffernan. Impressed by the youngster's athleticism, the coach was equally captured by his willingness to listen, work hard, and take as long as was necessary to get what he was told right.

Said Heffernan, "The first ever session I had with Ian, he said, "Let's just hit a few and see what we are working with." He hit me one forehand, stopped and said "Oh shit! What have they done to you?" with a sigh of disappointment. He didn't turn me down, instead insisting that he was going to make my forehand my weapon. Ian took it upon himself to discipline me. One time, I remember I lost a close match. That didn't bother him, but what did was the way I carried on and misbehaved, throwing my racquet, yelling out etc. After the match he took me round the back of the clubhouse and got so angry at me I nearly cried, saying that if I continued acting like that he wouldn't coach me anymore.

"When I was 12, Ian and Jackie took me to the Gold Coast for a training camp. I was expecting a couple of hours of hitting each day and then resting. This was not the case. Ian, despite his age, woke me up at 6 am and told me we were both going for a run. Not only did he keep the same pace as me, afterwards he came in the surf with me. Then we practised for around five hours of high intensity hitting. Not long after this training camp I won the 12 and Under national title, held in Mildura. At that age it is hard to appreciate how or why you won it, but I can basically attribute the win to Ian.

"Ian was always positive and passionate about my tennis. This created a great atmosphere for training and improving. His constant rants about "Move your bloody feet!" or "Ohhh, not the net, anywhere but the net" still haunt me to this day, which shows how powerful and how much his words meant to me. The way he went about his days and work influenced me and my practice and how hard I wanted to work. He taught us that short and sharp sessions were significantly more productive than long, tiring sessions. Yet, he still somehow knew when I was burnt out or run down, notifying Mum or Dad that I needed a rest.

"I guess Ian was like a grandfather for me growing up and someone who I always thought had the answers to everything. This came about due to his personal interest in my tennis game and also in my off-court activities, such as football. Ian was different to all other coaches for me because he came and watched every tournament and took notes so as after he could inform me of any mistakes or statistics that would help me moving forward in my next match or tournament." This was Barclay going to the nth degree.

With Jackie's health on the gradual decline, Heffernan's mother, Louise, and other parents of Ian's students often took meals across to the Barclay household to help out. Dr Shastra Naidu, mother of student Nish Morris, took on the role of doctor to Jackie, always graciously on call and often at short notice. Barclay's sister-in-law Kay continued to lend assistance to both with the household duties.

Official Appointments

Barclay's long-held dissatisfaction and occasional verbal stoushes with tennis' national- and state-governing bodies came to a head in the early 2000s. This time, rather than again berating the organisations about their narrow vision, self-interest, slowness in getting things done and historic lack of successful programs on behalf of junior tennis development, he was encouraged to put his money where his mouth was.

He did an about-turn and got involved. Tennis Victoria's active Player Development Manager, Elizabeth Peers, had recently helped initiate a new concept called Talent Identification Day (TID) from which both a boys' and girls' junior state squad was selected in the 12 and Under age group.

Targeted by Peers, Barclay took on the role of head coach for the girls' squad. The two discussed his wish to have two of the state's most energetic and keen female coaches, who had a great love of junior tennis, become involved.

Ann Quinn was available and an obvious choice. Qualified school teacher Belinda Colinari also got an opportunity, but was apprehensive about joining a doyen of tennis coaching. Her fears were quickly allayed. "Ian was very encouraging in promoting female coaches. There weren't many involved at the higher level of the junior game and he felt it necessary that they got on board where possible, particularly to help the young girls," she said.

Barclay's appointment lasted five years. In that time, he had what he describes as a lot of mini talent. "We had no one of great size, power or physical development to be a world beater, but we had some great triers." In his search for the best available teaching surface, his squad trained out of the Yarra Valley Country Club in Bulleen, which had Melbourne's traditional en tout cas surface.

The trio took his young squad on interstate trips for tournaments to help further their development. Colinari later took up Tennis Australia's Professional Development Co-ordinator role. She attributed the education she received on the game from Barclay during their time together, for helping her attain the position. "Ian mentored me in so many ways and continues to do so to this very day. He was also one of the first to arrive at my wedding."

Barclay had been a mentor for Steve Wood. Early in 2005, Wood sought counsel from Barclay when the position of Chief Executive Officer at Tennis Australia became vacant. Wood explained to Barclay that he'd already had a good run in his chosen technology industry, but tennis had been a sport he had played all his life. He had been an investor in it and realised the benefits that the game had for the community at large.

Tennis Australia was looking for help from a corporate-style professional businessman. He quizzed his ex-Linton Cup coach on whether he thought he should look at the opportunity. "Barkers told me it was the type of job I could certainly take on." He also consulted the coach on what he thought were the pressing issues within the game. Wood got his head around leaving a very successful corporate career to enter the not-for-profit, alternative style organisation.

He duly considered the exciting opportunity to give back to his sport and promptly convened a meeting which included Barclay and several of the country's leading tennis coaches. He posed questions to the group, such as what did Tennis Australia need to do to get more people playing more tennis, more often, for longer, to deliver Grand Slam champions and to make tennis the social fabric of the community? Did they agree and how should Tennis Australia go about it? Wood was successful in securing the CEO job at Tennis Australia and from day one in his new office, regularly kept counsel with Barclay on the same issues.

Recognition

Ironically, it was when, at age 68 in 2007, that Ian Barclay was finally acknowledged by his peers, being presented with a TCAV Coach of the Year award at Kooyong.

It was probably only then that his knowledge, experience and results began to be truly respected in his home country. He admits that 30 odd years previously, he was quite opposed to what the governing body of tennis coaching stood for. It's arguable now that back then Barclay could well have written the coaches' course himself, let alone be made to undertake it.

In June 2011, on the Queen's Birthday, Ian Barclay was awarded an Order of Australia Medal for services to the sport of tennis. It could well be argued that the wonderful recognition had long been coming for the coach who had put a mountain of runs on the board and given his life to the game he had loved dearly for nearly six decades. For Barclay it was a very humbling experience. "To give all these years of my heart and soul to the game, success in two countries, a lot of luck, wonderful support from Jackie and many, many great memories along the way, it's a very nice reward."

Tennis Victoria also recognised Barclay, awarding him the 2011/12 Victorian Spirit of Tennis Award, as an acknowledgement of his significant and valuable contribution to the advancement or popularity of the sport of tennis.

So too did Tennis Australia, as in 2012 it recognised Barclay by awarding him the President's Spirit of Tennis Award.

In 2013, at the annual TCAV awards night, Ian Barclay was inducted into the TCAV Hall of Fame. The same year, his beloved Hawthorn won the first of three successive AFL Premierships.

In December of 2016 at the TCAV's 60th birthday celebrations held at Kooyong, Ian Barclay was installed as the fourth coach into the Legend category, alongside other renowned Victorian coaches Don Tregonning, Ian Occleshaw (deceased) and Norman Cahill.

In keeping pace, for the last few years he has accompanied other TCAV coaches to the United States Professional Tennis Association's Conferences to extend his learning. He has fitted in like a glove and has been warmly looked after by all.

Ironically, the coaching establishment that in his early days he was so far removed from, these days embraces him like no other.

An About-Turn

From his very first 1979 European trip, Barclay continued, year after year, to ear bash anyone who would listen about the importance and benefits of introducing clay courts into Australia.

Several popped up at centres around Australia but nothing at National Headquarters.

At one stage in the early days Barclay proposed that the Ringwood Tennis Club, 30 kilometres from the city in Melbourne's eastern suburbs, situated close to a major freeway, be looked at as a potential venue. The club, with 10 en tout cas courts, had been used sparingly for many years. He believed it could have been re-laid with clay and turned into a super centre. No response.

Years later, and Tennis Australia has eight clay courts located at Melbourne Park.

Somewhat by chance, Barclay joined forces with Tennis Australia in 2009. He had penned an article in Australia's national monthly *Tennis* publication, which centred on the then looming election of office bearers at the pointy end of tennis' national body. He felt that with so much infighting and struggle for power taking place that those entrusted with overseeing the health and direction of tennis in Australia had lost much of their focus, in particular, toward his pet love – junior tennis development. He felt it didn't represent a good picture for the game.

Kim Kachel, son of ex-professional tour player and fellow coaching colleague of Barclay's, Chris Kachel, headed up Tennis Australia's Talent Search and Development department. In the midst of developing and improving its own programs and initiatives, it launched the Talent Development Coaches Program in late 2009 to recognise the passionate coaches who were getting good results with pupils at a national level, particularly in the 12 and Under age group.

Tennis Australia decided to appoint five national coach mentors. Kachel thought using Barclay as a mentor was a 'no brainer' when selections were made. His experience in the game could not be wasted anymore in his home country. Kachel had seen Barclay's influence on his students first hand years earlier.

As a neighbour of the Barclay family, a young Kachel often went over to the coach's court to be a hitting partner for a similarly young Andrew Thomas.

Kachel frequently left each practice session more educated about his own game than before he arrived.

Barclay's job description with Tennis Australia was to liaise with coaches at all the Australian 12 and 14 and Under Nationals' titles, to watch players' matches with them and provide feedback, give guidance, support and help lift the overall standard of coaching.

In Barclay's role, he constantly liaised with Kim Kachel. They would chew the fat over upcoming projects. Kachel often went over to Barclay's house at around 7.30 pm and rarely left before midnight. They had similar ideals and principles about the game.

Kachel said, "Ian was constantly looking for ways to increase and improve our tennis stocks. If he wasn't with me, he could be found in the office chatting with the Coach Development team or other departments about that very matter. Whenever I rang to enquire about his availability for an upcoming national junior event, time and time again he would be ready to go, not wanting to miss an opportunity to see the next batch of young prospects in action. If he couldn't get to a tournament, he would ring me to see how the kids had fared."

"At a national junior event played on the grass courts in Mildura in the north-west corner of regional Victoria, Ian made a presentation to those talent identification coaches who attended, on the topic of the serve, a stroke he is very passionate about. He was instantly attracted to any coach keen to produce good players, inexperienced or not."

"At age 73, he was still going at the crack of dawn to witness first up matches on courts still covered with morning dew, just to be on the lookout for emerging talent. Coaches from the major Australian cities and regional towns sent him videos of their pupils for technical and tactical advice, much like his British coaches did over a decade before. He believed developing a mass of young players was comparable to constructing a house. He wanted to build the base as wide and strong as possible, so as to prevent it from collapsing. He wouldn't turn anybody away," said Kachel. This was a further example of Barclay going to the nth degree.

Steve Wood and Ian Barclay often met for lunch at Melbourne Park. In Wood's words, "When he wanted lunch, that generally meant something was bothering Barkers. He would tell me how it was. He would say you have got to get this done or you are not executing in that area. We are doing well here but we need more resources there. I was delighted that he was willing to help out. He loved being out there, particularly with the younger kids, getting their technique right so that these players could have a career in the game. He was renowned for doing the extra work and his results spoke for themselves. He had some very strong beliefs that focused on a narrow part of the business that we ran at Tennis Australia and sometimes he struggled with that. When I sat with him and explained the complexity of what it is we did, from running a Grand Slam down to grassroots tennis, he understood, but his natural balance was to always go back to the young kids, to get them to enjoy the love of the game and if it wasn't done to his satisfaction, he was unhappy. And therefore he became anti-establishment and he would ring me up and give me a spray along those lines."

Wood thought Tennis Australia did a considerable amount in Barclay's domain. "Barkers would tell me we could always do more. He would also say to me, as was well known, the competitive landscape in searching for talented and committed young players was intense. Our organisation needed to be resourced correctly and organised appropriately to play its part in the big competitive sporting arena. Barkers knew that and because he was so passionate about junior tennis he banged on about it to the point where it sometimes got painful. Some people told him to put up or shut up, but that's just Barkers and I'm happy to say that's who he was, that's what he is about and that can never be questioned because the die was cast on what he believed and he is unwavering on that commitment and ideal. He would also have to be one of the fittest 70-plus-year-olds going around and potentially a very dangerous player on the ITF world 70 and Over circuit if he was ever to tour."

Wood had long been aware of Barclay's issue with the state of Australian tennis courts. "Barkers loves clay courts and he did an immense amount of work on his own backyard court to make sure it was one of the best in the country. Those who had the privilege to play on it, together with the beautiful surrounds, know how great a place it is to play tennis. He believed that his court taught one how to hit shots far better than synthetic grass courts. He was very worried that solid stroke technique production could fall away, given the volume of synthetic grass courts around. More and more courts popped up and it concerned him greatly. Tennis Australia did everything possible to get more clay courts, but had big challenges with sustainability and maintenance of that type of courts. Even when we laid the French or Italian style of courts in the harsh environments of Australia, with all the maintenance necessary, it still didn't give us the result we wanted, which was to have a clay court which is sustainable. We put around 68 clay court facilities around Australia which got up and running, but in Barkers' view, it wasn't enough. He wanted more."

Barclay continued to work seven days a week, both privately at home as well as for Tennis Australia. Through luck, continual work, or the good grace from above, his body continued to hold up well after 40 years of professional tennis coaching. Only then did he start to have some concerns and in 2010 he tore his plantar fascia. Typically stubborn, after being told to rest, he continued to coach and would do so for up to six hours a day. This subsequently caused some knee problems from favouring one side. "I've done all the wrong things for my body, but perhaps because I've worked hard all my life, it doesn't know anything else. It just keeps going," he said at the time.

As Barclay sat in his chair after yet another long day, he turned on the television to watch a video of yet another junior whose game he was rebuilding. This time it was a young 10-year-old boy from Vanuatu. He had just won his first junior tournament. Barclay delighted in his progress, yet at the same time was wary, as the child's pedigree didn't augur well for him being very tall. It didn't matter that much, Barclay was just happy to see another young charge improve his tennis.

In late November the same year, Barclay went back to London to visit daughter Toni-Ann and her family. He once again caught up with his old friends.

Nick Brown took him to the London ATP Masters Doubles finals event. The Brit had been coaching Polish players Marius Frystenberg and Marin Matkowski, who had made it into the end-of-year top eight for the round-robin format. Ironically the night Barclay left, the pair defeated the American world number-one-ranked pair of Bob and Mike Bryan, to then go on to reach the semi-finals and a number four world ranking. Brown felt proud to share the win with his great Australian mentor and friend.

During the Easter of 2011, Barclay again linked up with Rocky Loccisano. Barclay's time included helping Loccisano conduct a tennis clinic on the Mediterranean island of Sardinia, off the coast of Italy. A full day of coaching was often followed by a night of great conversation, centred on Barclay

Super 10s Junior Tennis

Barclay was then at the forefront of a new idea. He felt there was a gap in the system in the 10 and Under age bracket for those juniors at the higher end of competition tennis. His idea to find more good competitors was born from the concept that had been used in the UK while he was based at Bisham Abbey. About 30 tennis centres from around the counties ran individual 10 and Under team competitions. Results were sent back to Bisham and county coaches would identify talent that warranted having a further look at.

Barclay talked at length with Kachel at Tennis Australia about creating a new similar competition. He talked again and again. Nothing happened in the short term and his patience was yet again tested.

Gradually Barclay's innovative idea became a reality and a new Super 10s age group team's competition rolled out at the Dendy Park Tennis Club in Brighton, Melbourne in 2012.

One hundred young boys and girls from all around came together under Barclay's watchful eye to try out for team positions. Twenty-four girls and 36 boys were chosen. The format allowed for players to play a singles and doubles match over two 50-minute sessions, with 10 minutes allocated for change overs. This allowed parents the opportunity to either stay and watch, or commit themselves to other family activities.

A five-week season was set aside together with finals. A coach was appointed to manage each team. Barclay believed the format would help the girls in particular stay together as in netball and feel a real team environment. Rewards were on offer to participants. One allowed a player to toss the coin at the Australian Open finals. Of those more over-indulgent parents, Barclay made a point of reminding them on leaving the complex every week, to make sure they told their kids how much they loved them, rather than being unnecessarily harsh after the day's play was complete.

Over the moon with the Super 10s inception, but still not content, Barclay wanted to spread the word. Year on year the numbers seeking to trial for positions grew, all attempting each time to impress selectors. Of course, Barclay wanted more, knowing how aggressive other mainstream sports worked to entice young children to participate. He continued to talk to Kachel.

Two years on, and Bendigo and Traralgon, major regional Victorian towns, were granted rights to operate their own Super 10s series. He knew how many champions came from country regions and how the surface had only been scratched in the 8-12 age bracket. It would also help to lessen the travel for many prospective players.

Given the chance and more venues, he would have doubled the number. Barclay was indebted to the hard work put in by Kim Kachel, who went interstate to help develop the Super 10s concept on a national level. During his involvement, Barclay would often find current or previous players from the Super 10s playing in any one of the tournaments he visited. It was the result he was after.

Barclay regularly attended Tennis Australia's two 8 and Under years of age Talent Identification days, held at Melbourne Park each year, always hopeful of seeking from it prospective Super 10s candidates.

The Biggest Loss

Ian with wife and soulmate, Jackie

On Saturday 21st July 2012, just short of their 50th wedding anniversary, Ian Barclay's staunchest ally, best friend, mother of their three children and grandmother to the three youngest men in their lives, wife Jackie passed away.

It had come after a long battle with emphysema and other related illnesses which she had contracted towards the end of their stay in London many years earlier. Jackie had fought for over 12 years.

As is well known, the life of a professional tennis coach's wife is not necessarily an easy one. A busy tennis coach can work from the early hours of the morning often until late into the evening, periods not conducive to good family time spent together. Ian Barclay has always been in that mould.

Fortunately, Jackie understood the industry, embraced it and became a vital cog in the Barclay coaching wheel. She welcomed everyone into the family's Mitcham, Park Orchards and London homes for the best part of 40 years.

She would cook breakfast, lunch and dinner for the never-ending production line of individual tennis players or groups who stayed, whether that be for a day, a week or sometimes even months. If Ian cursed a live-in student because he thought they hadn't completed their school homework or filled out a tournament entry form on time, they generally just giggled back. Jackie always came to their rescue.

If any child was lacking a little in manners, she was on to it. She looked after Ian's tribe of juniors' travel arrangements whenever they flew off interstate or overseas. She always double-checked that tennis bags were packed and made sure nothing was left to chance when a new tournament was to be contested.

Alongside her husband, she chaperoned countless young tennis players away to tournaments around the country and the world, giving love and encouragement, sometimes advice and even the odd backhander where needed.

If sponsorship patches needed to be sewn onto tennis shirts to adhere to contractual commitments, Jackie attended to it. She, like Ian, wanted each child he took on to grow as a person, not just as a tennis player. She remained staunchly loyal of Ian or any family member who was ridiculed or attacked by sections of the media or others from within, or outside the tennis community.

Pat Cash received his fair share of negative media over the years. Jackie would have none of it. Whenever Ian was away from home on tennis duties, Jackie was the rock for the rest of the family.

She was able to raise their three children, Dean, Brad and Toni-Ann, as well as any mother could in such circumstances. Without her, it is doubtful Ian could have achieved what he did.

She was unique. Being a sibling to her tough younger footballing brother Jimmy, she had always demonstrated a likeminded competitive streak.

Doing crosswords and puzzles were some of her favourite pastimes. She was staunchly supportive of her children and taught them that any junior who walked through their household door knew the importance of competing, fighting for what's right and always having a go. Through watching Ian coach and the many matches his pupils played, she also developed a keen eye for the game. She could pick up on styles and tactics being used and therefore was yet another set of eyes that could be called on when help was needed.

On the other hand, she also possessed the beautiful gift of compassion, a quality shared by her devoted younger sister Kay. In her union with Ian, she brought both qualities to their tennis life together. From the time he stepped onto the court for his first stint as a full-time professional tennis coach at the Heatherdale Tennis Club in 1973, Jackie was the left hand to Ian's right.

As her illness gradually took its toll, Jackie was more and more restricted to staying at home. It didn't stop her keeping a keen eye on the horse racing both for herself, Ian, Dean and Brad. She religiously did the daily newspaper crossword, kept up her passion for reading books, watched sport and her favourite shows on television and still attended to all the household bills.

Her long-standing Heatherdale Tennis Club friends continued to visit and take her out for monthly lunches.

At a beautiful funeral service held for Jackie Barclay in the peaceful surrounds of Wattle Park in Melbourne's eastern suburbs, before a gathering of over 300 family members, close friends and many from the tennis community, the three children fondly recalled their mother's undeniable influence on so many people who came into Barclay's family life and her wonderful gifts of life to each and every one.

Of his mother Brad said, "Jackie the 'den' mother, was a special person. She was a lioness for us and all the other tennis kids, supporting everyone under almost any circumstance. In her life with Dad, she put up with all the things that went on with the tennis territory, but the life itself enriched her. Their relationship was always loving. They argued and still did up until Mum's passing, but their unity was always so strong. Dad has always been happy just to have $50 in his wallet, a little to bet on at the races and bit to have a beer with. I don't think Dad has ever paid a bill in his life.

"Mum was always the bookkeeper. In their early years travelling overseas, she always made sure we were left in good hands."

Flying Solo Again

Barclay gradually became tired and somewhat disillusioned with the inner workings at Tennis Australia.

On a day-to-day basis, he saw a growing number of new employees, high on academic and business skills, but short on tennis knowledge, put on. The establishment appeared more and more to resemble a 9 am – 5 pm working mentality. For him, that in itself became a worrying sign.

Eventually, in early 2017, Barclay, aged 78, decided to leave his post and continue to work solely from his Park Orchards home court, keeping a close eye on his ever-evolving batch of private pupils. Although recompensed by the organisation, no value could possibly be put on the effort, devotion and endless hours he had contributed during his tenure at the national body's headquarters.

Barclay's experience at Tennis Australia reaffirmed his belief that junior tennis in Australia drastically needs a rebirth, believing the establishment has struggled to really hit the sweet spot in the delicate relationship between itself, coaches and the great potential of the many young players within the community.

At the elite level, where millions of dollars are poured into players, coaches and administrators, Barclay points out that only five Australian players – Pat Cash, Pat Rafter, Lleyton Hewitt, Sam Stosur and most recently Ashleigh Barty – have truly had success at the top echelons of the singles game over the last three decades.

Barclay is concerned that in future years, because the landscape has changed so much, there could be very few of the nation's home-grown product playing in the Australian Open and other Grand Slam junior events.

He feels the introduction of more money and ranking points' tournaments has played its part in changing the dynamic of junior tennis.

"Many young juniors are chasing points, playing only in tournaments, and don't belong to a local club. They are therefore not having to respond to the challenge of playing regularly in a team and don't get the benefits of playing doubles. So many are playing in the senior money tournaments on offer at such a young age, that they are forgoing the junior pathway."

He cites the 12 and Under age group as a prime example "The introduction of points into the 12 and Under age group caused a major problem. Instead of development, the system created a negative situation for young boys and girls. Very young juniors wouldn't play shots. Just pushing the ball became paramount and the moon ball became their basic shot. 12 and Under tennis became negative, with no shot making.

"It also created a new form of tournament dodging, which meant the best players in the age group very often didn't oppose each other, other than in nationals.

"In the early days where there was no age limit in the AMT's (Australian Money Tournaments), many 12-year-olds entered, hoping to meet someone of the same birth year, as winning a first round of an AMT would give them more points than going further in their own age group draw. This greatly affected the numbers and standard in the mainstream 12 and Under age group. Some 12-year-olds would go so far as to wait till the eleventh hour to enter a tournament for fear of losing to someone they felt they could not beat. Super 10s was a better standard because no pressure was applied to the younger age group.

"This is also reaffirmed by the fact that it is mostly only the wealthy that can afford to travel and compete in many major points tournaments. Unfortunately, many super athletes, who are a bit rough around the edges and from a different socio economic background, never get that opportunity.

"People who are in positions of selecting national squads and teams are only concerned about how many points have been accumulated through the year and not at other potential that doesn't get looked at. This change has in a way backfired on the development of junior tennis. No one seems to have come up with a real answer."

He agonisingly sees stagnation in his beloved sport in his own state and cites several reasons for it. Many smaller clubs have gone, only to be replaced with housing estates or commercial buildings. Many that do still exist are in poor condition, with minimal finance or help available to upgrade facilities. Sundays, once a major social and competitive playing day, sadly sees many courts being under-utilised. Club volunteers have become scarcer and much harder to find.

Barclay feels his beloved Super 10s project had largely been neglected by those at the top, with only meagre funds allocated for its promotion. Apart from Kim Kachel's heavy contribution towards its development, little advertising meant limited knowledge. Five years into the competition and Barclay came across coaches and clubs who had never heard of the concept. If they had received a generic Tennis Australia email, it could easily have been dismissed, not passed on by secretaries or read by coaches.

Barclay believes the reluctance and lack of interest in having more Super 10s centres, particularly in country regions that could widen the base of the structured pyramid and bring more seven, eight, nine and 10-year-olds into the frame, has only added to the sports ever-diminishing numbers. It has potentially lessened the numbers dovetailing out of Hot Shots programs. In his mind, its overall growth therefore had been small.

An added issue for Barclay, and a problem he sees, is the reluctance of many coaches to spend the extra necessary hours on court to make improvements. "Money has become the most important feature in coaching, not creating great players for the future. The other huge concern is that very few coaches attend tournaments to watch how their pupils perform under pressure. Young players do not do in matches what they do on the practice court. Training and coaching are worlds apart from tough competition.

"My observations are that it has degenerated even further over the last couple of years. This problem has contributed to slowing progress of junior development even further. Many of our young players are tactically inept, as they have not been taught how to construct a point. In the eyes of many, caring for pupils and their futures has been a thing of the past and to seek technical and tactical perfection is fading fast."

Ian Barclay, still wholeheartedly devoted to junior tennis development, desperately wants his sport to prosper. He knows that the wider the base of the pyramid at the participation level, the more young players there are to develop. Maybe one even into another Wimbledon champion.

On that scale, Barclay believes doing away with rankings points in the 12 and Under age group and focusing solely on development would go some way to helping the situation. He would love to see coaches of his ilk employed by Tennis Australia to go to all the junior tournaments specifically to spot talent.

In 2010, a National Coach Mentoring scheme was set up to help our young coaches, particularly during national junior titles.

Aside from Barclay, those involved were Rob Kilderry, Gary Stickler, Bill Bowrey and Nicole Arendt. "The panel had a wealth of experience, between them having coached an incredible amount of national and international champions. To pass on their knowledge of the game, some coaches found it invaluable."

Having always believed in the value of clay courts in junior development, Barclay believes the national titles, hosted at venues such as Ipswich in Queensland, are of great value because the event is played on clay and gives the best indication of the most talented and competitive players the country has.

If promoted better, he still sees a great opportunity for Tennis Australia's Hot Shots and other short tennis programs dovetailing into his baby, the Super 10s program. With this in place, only then does he truly believe that tennis can compete in the market place with other sports.

Australian Rules football for both boys and girls, cricket, soccer, netball, and basketball are examples of sports that are now not only well entrenched within the community, but have sizeable amounts of money poured into their diverse grassroots junior development programs.

He would love to see more creative thinkers emerge from within the governing body to search for ways to provide for the country's young talent. On his time working for Tennis Australia, Barclay simply enjoyed giving something back to the game, that for so long had given him so much. The love of being involved with each new generation of children and their coaches stood above all.

Continuing the Dream

As the years pass, Ian Barclay continually keeps up with the ever-changing tennis landscape and moves with the times.

Out on the tennis court, he has seen his fair share of young players with extreme western grips on the forehand side. He sees one downside, that being an inability to get the ultra-closed racquet face underneath an oncoming short wide ball.

He recalls witnessing firsthand many years earlier when his young English protégé, James Trotman, repeatedly used a short inside-out sliced backhand against Russian Nikolay Davydenko during the International Junior Sunshine Cup in Florida to exploit the weakness.

And wait for it – yes – another young player emerged from under Barclay's wing, extremely talented Melbourne left-hander, Aidan Vaughan.

On seeing the boy firsthand, the coach saw something different. His keen eye zeroed in on the talented youngster's hands, his great feel for the ball and all-round ability. Having already captured a 12 and Under national title, Vaughan continued to give hope to his coach. On changing a western grip on his forehand drive back to a semi-western grip, Barclay gleaned when the boy took the changes like a duck to water.

After some surgery, Barclay has recovered and is keen to get back to the courts and watch his 14-year-old charge, Vaughan, play a semi-final of a 16 and Under singles rankings event at Boroondara. As I sit with him in an enclosed gazebo behind a back court out of the cold, I know after a 44-year relationship with Barkers, I myself will yet again come away from the experience more educated.

Early in the first set it is easy to feel the coach's passion. Comments start to flow as to how the two have spent hours working on things, but few are being done well. Young Vaughan is missing badly when the ball is hit to him down the centre of the court. Barkers berates his poor use of footwork. He is not getting any first serves in or winning the first point of any game. In-between points he turns to quickly watch a young female junior playing on an adjacent court, who he is also coaching.

Barclay turns back to Vaughan and gives him a gesture to move more, then sighs, shakes his head, then in an instant applauds a massive inside-out cross-court forehand that the opponent can't get near.

He tells me that when his young charge has his mind on the job, he can produce anything. He wants Vaughan to toss the ball higher on serve as he is dumping too many into the net. He notes the opponent is mis-hitting forehands, struggling to cope with the crosswind. Barkers plays every point. Coach and student making eye contact, the youngster smiling after a point won, but poorly played. He wants the boy to use his top hand more, to generate more power on his double-hand backhand, but admits he is toying with the idea of changing the shot to a single hand only. Barkers tells me the boy is still only 14 years, but immature compared to the likes of Cash and Hartnett of a bygone era at the same age. He needs to continue to be patient through the ups and downs of the boy's development.

Vaughan does enough to win the first set 6-4. The coaching roller-coaster quickly returns as the second set commences and Vaughan loses the first point cheaply. Barkers' temperature rises sharply as he reminds me how often he has spoken to Vaughan about getting off to a strong start at the beginning of a new set. From there, young Vaughan gets on a roll and takes the set and the match comfortably. Youngsters and parents drop into the gazebo to say hello to Barclay let him know how they've gone in their own matches, come in for some advice or to get a time for their next lesson. This is Ian Barclay going to the nth degree.

During each of the school holidays, yet again he watches junior tournaments the entire time. Well known to so many, parents often come up to ask questions, query a child's next move up the tennis chain or just quiz him about the state of the game. He is a magnet.

The year 2017 marked the 30th anniversary of Patrick Cash's Wimbledon victory. Barclay was there in London to celebrate, reflect, and be there with old friends and his family. Without fanfare, they charged glasses at a local wine bar in Fulham.

He also caught up with his Bisham Abbey connections, where celebrations were livelier. A school bus was hired to take the group on a pub crawl around Marlowe. The coach reminisced with old students Martin Lee, James Trotman, Lee Childs and Simon Dickson, assistant coaches Jimmy Turner and Phil Fowler, with girls' squad players Laura Austin and Zoe Mellis.

As always, he took careful note during the second week of the Grand Slam event how the latest crop of the world's best juniors were performing. He didn't let the opportunity go, however, to get away from the courts of Wimbledon to watch his grandson Austin train in the Chelsea 10 and Under academy soccer squad.

As the US Open rolls around, Barclay agonised that no Australian junior made it into the Boys' or Girls' Singles draws.

Barclay duly notes how much taller many of the boys and girls in the tennis world have become. He sees bigger serves and shorter rallies, not convinced that the style of play always shows a great spectacle.

He is amazed at the power being generated by the younger women on the main tour. He cites 2017 French Open Singles winner, Latvian Jelena Ostapenko, as an example. Many players now have footwork experts on hand to help them. Over 50 years of this religious practice of watching tennis at the highest level has shown him how the game has changed so much.

At the end of the year, Barclay undertook a trip to the US and spent a couple of weeks with Vaughan and his other top students, Shyan Sivaratnam and Jessie Burbridge, for some intense training with Rohan Goetzke at the IMG centre in Florida in December in preparation for the Tennis Australia showdown back at Melbourne Park,

Burbridge said of Barclay, "We embarked on a tennis trip to the IMG Tennis Academy in Florida on 3rd December 2017. There were four tennis-aspiring students and Ian was super enthusiastic for someone who has travelled with juniors so many times all across the world in previous years. While we missed the third flight and the first day of training, we had the most wonderful and enjoyable experience with the most incredible coach. IMG was memorable. We are so grateful and privileged for Ian being there with us. Not only was he a coach dedicated to travel to the academy halfway across the world, but he was very dedicated day in and day out, helping us to improve our tennis skills. Every single night he gave us feedback for the day's work and you could see his passion for the sport shining through. We will never forget the time Barkers was called Rim by the Starbucks waiter or the moment where he unleashed on the boys for missing a training session on their day off. But you will always be the winner when it comes to the most chocolate milk drank in two weeks, outlasting all of us. Most importantly, we enjoyed ourselves. Special thanks to Rohan, Ian's long-time friend, for helping us make the trip possible. The experience was filled with many laughs and constant smiles and it was an experience all four of us will never forget. Thank you, Ian."

Influences in UK

Several of Barclay's ex-British contingent of boys have continued to remain actively involved in the game.

Nick Brown coached the British Federation Cup team from 1998-2003, was Poland's Davis Cup and Olympic coach, coached Cambridge University's men's and ladies' teams and held a position of technical consultant to the LTA. When after yet another regime change, the LTA came back to Brown and asked if he would work with some of the younger children in their talent identification program in the south east London area, Brown decided to get back involved in the national junior tennis system, because like Barclay before him, he genuinely cared about the game of tennis in the UK and cared about the young up-and-coming prospects who had dreams.

As well as his on-court demands, Brown also did some commentary for television's *Eurosport*, which he found not only fun but kept him tuned to what was happening at the top of the sport. "In my eyes, having coached myself and spent many years around some of the world's most successful coaches, Barkers was the best of the best, particularly in respect of the technical side of the game, able to take a player's game to pieces and totally rebuild it if necessary."

James Turner continued to work for the LTA for a time, both in Bath and Leeds, before taking on roles as High Performance Coach at Ilkley Tennis and Squash Club and then Head Coach at Bramhall Lane Lawn Tennis Club. He often reminded himself of a phrase Barclay told him, "You are only as good as your last lesson." He knew that if he had a good, productive lesson with his players one day, the next one needed to be better if any progress was to be made. Commitment, selflessness, and devotion to his job are traits he absorbed from his one-time mentor. Like any coach, as Turner has found, those qualities bring with it challenges to one's own life and relationships, but he learned much about the professionalism needed to have any form of success at the highest level. He still pushes his charges hard like he did at Bisham Abbey, but having learned from Barclay fun is still the foremost ingredient.

Phil Fowler also continued with the LTA as a touring coach, before landing at Wimbledon. He stayed there for two years, which included taking on a Federation Cup coaching role. That was followed by a13-year stint as Head Coach at Stoke Park Country Club, Spa and Hotel, before a stint at Martin Lee's Living Tennis and now working for himself as a Consultant Coach. He learned much from Barclay in his time at Bisham and his messages to students have invariably reflected those of his former mentor, such as "treat the court as your real estate and protect it at all costs! Make the baseline your best friend! Never, ever go near the net with a shot!" Being tough when needed, but at the same time nurturing and making students feel special was a Barclay way. Fowler has never forgotten.

After retiring from the tour in 2006, due mainly to injuries, Martin Lee coached at Bisham with a private company called WinTennis. In 2012, he became involved in another coaching business as a co-director, called Living Tennis, in partnership with Paul, Jamie and Johnny Delgado. The organisation runs its Pro Academy out of Bisham Abbey. The ex-academy pupil and former number-one-ranked junior in the world has helped look after some of his own country's best prospects. He still takes much of Barclay on court with him as he educates and helps his own charges on their tennis journey.

James Trotman commenced his coaching journey in Spain, before becoming a travelling hitting coach for professional players on behalf of the LTA. He then spent five years Down Under as a high performance coach with Tennis Australia, overseeing and travelling with players such as Sam Groth and Greg Jones in its post-junior program. At the time, he saw very talented players transition into his domain, trying to get a foothold onto the professional tour. His biggest concern lay in the deficiencies he saw in his players' doubles skills, particularly when their volleys were put to the test. Having spent so much time at Bisham Abbey in his junior days under Barclay, honing his own doubles skills, he remained unsure how much attention was being paid to the net game at the grassroots level in his temporary adopted country.

After leaving Australia, Trotman had a stint with highly ranked English male, Kyle Edmund. He currently is the LTA Consultant Coach, overlooking the programs for elite players transitioning into the top 100 rankings. He has never forgotten Barclay's influence on himself and these days his own coaching. "Barkers the person, his work ethic, his treatment of everyone around him, his humility, love and passion for his sport has always impacted on me and will always be front and centre in my mind."

Lee Childs retired from professional tennis in 2007. He spent time coaching alongside Phil Fowler at Stoke Park Country Club. Going on to coach full-time back at the Queen's Club, he would often hear himself repeating words Barclay had said to him as a junior, such as "go back behind the opposition with that shot!", "stay as loose as a goose!", or "get down to the low volleys!" The young coach stuck to what he learned from his mentor because he knew it worked. He looked for a time when he could get Barclay back to have a look at some of his own young protégés. After eight years as the Head Professional, Childs took on the role as the Queen's Club's Head of Lawn Tennis. Childs also currently holds the position of Head of Development at the nearby Effingham Schools Tennis Academy, which is jointly held at local schools, St Teresa's and Cranmore, in Effingham, Surrey. There he sets programs and session plans for students at the Academy.

Another successful Bisham Abbey junior of Barclay's, Daniel Kiernan, also turned to coaching. In going on to eventually become Britain's number-one-ranked doubles player, these days Kiernan heads up the busy Soto Tennis Academy in Sotogrande, Spain. Often in contact with his former coach, he waits for the day Barclay can visit the highly rated centre, perhaps with another group of the elder statesman's up-and-coming protégés.

Following in Their Mentor's Footsteps

Several of Barclay's top Australian juniors, who had tried their hand on the professional tour for a number of years, began to follow in their mentor's footsteps and branched out into professional coaching careers.

Returning to Australia after several years away based in Switzerland, Mark Hartnett set up his own Pro Tennis Academy at the Donvale Tennis Club. He married girlfriend Lisa Keller and they moved to Park Orchards, not far from Barclay. They built a tennis court in their own backyard, where they too conducted lessons. Hartnett attained a High Performance coaching accreditation in 1992.

Daniel Carroll returned to Melbourne and played high-level local pennant tennis before taking on the head coaching position at the Blackburn Tennis Club.

Wes Horskins set up his Futures Tennis Academy, based out of the East Malvern Tennis Club, Barclay's old stomping ground.

Rocky Loccisano based himself in Duisburg, Germany, where he still lives. There, he established a successful tennis coaching business, at the same time raising four boys with his wife, Enis, the boys all tennis players. Two sons, Ben and Mike, now compete on the lower levels of the ATP World Tour, while the other two boys keep an interest in the sport.

Rohan Goetzke's coaching story has been a journey in itself. He remained in Europe and linked up with the Belgium Tennis Federation. There he was based at the Lovanium Tennis Club as an assistant Head Coach. Two or three times a week he conducted regional coaching in the Brabant District, situated in the Dutch-speaking side of Belgium. At the conclusion of his tenure, he made a short trip back to Australia, before heading back to Europe and playing some club matches in Germany. Although still living in Belgium, he then took on a role on behalf of the Dutch Federation as a travelling coach with the country's best young players, the likes of Richard Krajicek, Jan Siemerink and Jacco Eltingh.

Goetzke's coaching journey then progressed to much greater heights. From 1993, he coached and travelled exclusively with Dutchman Richard Krajicek.

Rohan Goetzke with Richard Krajicek in 1996

Both player and coach put their names on the map on the biggest stage at Wimbledon in 1996 when Krajicek, seeded 17th, unexpectedly won the Wimbledon Men's Singles, defeating American MaliVai Washington in the final 6-3, 6-4, 6-3.

He had defeated former champion Michael Stich in the fourth round and then American legend Pete Sampras in the quarter-final along the way.

Barclay was over the moon with Goetzke's achievement. The young coach had first taken on Krajicek when the Dutchman was 16 years of age. Like his own mentor Barclay, he had seen something special in a young player that made it worth persevering with. Similarly, he had ridden the ups and downs with his young player as had Barclay with Pat Cash. Krajicek had a love/hate relationship with grass courts and after playing poorly at Rosemalen on the eve of Wimbledon he and Goetzke came close to moving in opposite directions. Having reached the final, both had to then deal with the sudden expectation of being the favourite against a lower-ranked player. As much as exultation, Goetzke felt relief.

Goetzke continued to shine on the world's coaching stage. Having parted ways with Dutchman Richard Krajicek after 10 years and with a career-high singles ranking of 4, Goetzke then coached the highly touted Croatian Mario Ancic. In their time together, along with a number of tour victories, the 6'5" tall Ancic made the semi-final of the 2004 Wimbledon Men's Singles.

In late October 2005, Goetzke became National Head Coach of the Dutch Tennis Federation. In early 2007, he was appointed Technical Director, as well as taking on stints as both the country's Davis Cup and Federation Cup Coach.

Having been involved with the Dutch Tennis Federation for well over a decade, in May of 2012, much to Barclay's delight, Goetzke took on the major role of Director at IMG's Bollittierri Tennis Academy in Florida, US, responsible for 45 coaches and over 300 junior players.

Interests, Friends and Family

Those who have known Ian Barclay well understand his need to both keep active and keep an active interest in all that goes on around him.

Horse racing has never been far from Barclay's mind. During one early pennant final, umpired by well-regarded local official, Max Atkins, Barclay cheekily carried a small transistor radio in the pocket of his shorts, with the racing channel switched on. Thinking the noise was coming from the crowd, Atkins turned to politely ask for silence. Shortly after, Barclay went up for a smash. Embarrassingly, the radio fell out of his pocket, landed at his feet and on breaking apart, batteries flew across the court in every direction.

One of Barclay's dreams outside of tennis came to bare. In the mid-1970s he bought into his first racehorse, by getting involved in a four-man syndicate that purchased a less-than-healthy two-year-old at a dispersal sale. At a cost of only $400, it was called *Golden Navel* and was looked after in the Victorian regional town of Ballarat by a young trainer, just starting out in the industry called Robert Smerdon.

Son Brad enjoyed going to the track with his father to watch it train. It was an interest, environment and opportunity he could share away from the tennis court. On the one-hour journey to Ballarat, the car radio was routinely tuned into the racing station. The horse performed well and won several races in Ballarat, at Moonee Valley and at Flemington on Melbourne Cup Day. It was a trier and in the end didn't owe the tennis coaching part owner a cent.

In 1980, Barclay got involved with another racehorse. The syndicate he joined, which also included Heatherdale court maintenance caretaker Jack Hayes, leased a two-year-old thoroughbred named *Bold Disco*. It won a first-up race in South Australia, defeating the horse of the year *Top of the Ladder*. It won two city races and a number of country races. Barclay had high hopes for his second acquisition. On entering the high-stakes Group 2, Karrakatta Plate, held over 1200 metres at Ascot in Perth, the horse started favourite and got out to a two-furlong lead, before fading. Back in the stable it developed scours. Barclay feared possible foul play, thinking it may have been interfered with. The disappointment of the horse's demise made him reluctant to take on another horse for some time.

After completing secondary school, Dean Barclay studied Primary School Teaching, firstly in Bendigo, then in Melbourne. Part of the way through his course, he acquired a job at the Mount Scopus Memorial College in Burwood. Courtesy of his physical education background, he worked in the school's sport department and took on the role of tennis coach, a job he held for the next three years.

Toni-Ann Barclay commenced her tertiary education, studying Architecture at Deakin University's regional campus in Geelong. Her parents bought her a house nearby to live in. After completing three years of her degree, she then deferred and in 1991 went to London to live with her parents. She got a job coaching tennis at the Riverside Club in Chiswick, London.

On his return to Australia from living in London, Brad Barclay made use of the electronic technician qualification he had completed at tertiary level and proceeded to work as a motor mechanic. He married his girlfriend, Vicki Morgan.

Ian cared for his charges and his friends who formed part of the extended family and experienced his care and devotion. While in London, Barclay's great mate from Melbourne, Barry Brennan took ill, to the point where he nearly died. On realising his friend was seriously unwell, Barclay rang each day for an update on his health. Brennan's wife Margaret couldn't believe the regularity of the calls from overseas and the concern from such a friend.

Toni-Ann Barclay returned to Australia to complete her BA, then Masters in Architecture. She then worked as an architect for a leading Melbourne firm and took to redesigning the five bedrooms in the Park Orchards family home, project managing the entire job.

She made a second trip across to London to see her parents in 1999 and travelled around to several of the junior tournaments with her father.

When back in Australia, the Barclays bought into yet another horse, called *Trust N Betrayal*. Barclay thought it was that slow he could beat it on foot. It was trained by one-time top tennis player and pennant contemporary, Ernie Ewart. The horse placed at several meetings, without ever landing him a big win.

Barclay continued to watch his beloved Hawthorn on weekends, play golf with his mates at the Commonwealth Golf Club and occasionally head to Flemington Racecourse to lay a few bets.

He received a phone call during the middle of 2004. His early tennis journey with Adelaide coaching counterpart Jan MacDonald had entrenched many friendships. He had always offered his help to anyone in any way if ever it was needed. Mike Webster was one parent whose son had been one of MacDonald's juniors in the early years. Both MacDonald's and Webster's sons later went on to gain scholarships at American universities. MacDonald's daughter was getting married in Copenhagen, Denmark. Webster was duly invited and as the wedding was to be held around the time of Wimbledon he thought he would try and tack on a visit to the tennis hallowed turf as well.

Webster was involved in the horse racing industry and had contacts all around the world. He sought out an acquaintance in the upper echelons of the industry in Britain in the hope of getting a ticket to the tennis, but the contact fell through. The licensed bookmaker thought of Barclay and rang, asking the coach if there was any chance of getting a ticket on Women's semi-final day, offering in exchange to help Barclay with tips on the weekly races in Adelaide. Barclay's cheeky reply was, "You don't want much, do you?"

In no time at all the ticket was sorted. It was typical Barclay. The two continued to indulge in their weekly Saturday racing telephone exchange. Another horse, named *Dr Generosity* entered the Barclay stable. It won a handful of country race meets to continue the family's interest in the sport.

Ian walks daughter Toni-Ann to be married

In 2005, Toni-Ann Barclay came out to Australia with her fiancé Tom where they married on the 19th March with a beautiful ceremony on the banks of the iconic Murray River at The Port of Echuca, in front of family and friends.

From there the entire wedding party and guests boarded the historic paddle steamer *Pevensy* for a ride down the Murray River to the reception, held at the well-known Oscar W's *Wharfside* restaurant and *Red Gum Grill & Deck Bar*.

Great Echuca family friend, Kaye Wearne, was instrumental in organising much of the day.

In 2007, Ian and Jackie became grandparents for the first time. London-based daughter Toni-Ann and husband Tom presented them with grandson, Austin.

Son Brad and his wife Vicky also delivered a grandson, Addison, born in 2008. A year later, a third grandson, Rafer, was born in the UK. Becoming grandparents gave both a new lease of life. "Dad and Mum got cranky if we didn't bring Addison over for the regular weekend visit," said Brad. "If I ran late, there would be a guaranteed phone call from Grandpa eager to know our whereabouts."

Ian Barclay's life is filled with many, many friends. He still takes a great interest in the worldly travels his sister Janet takes each year. On Monday nights he has dinner at one-time top junior Warren Brennan and his wife Katrina Kearney's home in Hawthorn. With Toni-Ann living abroad, Katrina's value to him is like that of having a second daughter. She has continually looked after and kept an eye on him. Their sons, Angus and Josh, always greet him with, "How are you going, old man?"

These days he is in constant contact with Toni-Ann and her husband Tom in London and checks in on grandsons Austin, Rafer and Addison as often as he can. He has kept supporting and still attends his beloved Hawthorn Football Club's games during the winter with son Brad. A keen soccer enthusiast, he attends hometown professional side Melbourne Victory's home games with Martin Kozma during the AFL off-season.

In May each year, he ventures to the annual Warrnambool Cup races in the country for three days with former squash-playing mate Barry O'Reilly and others. That generally means plenty of bets and beverages.

Yet again, Barclay has another interest in a racehorse. The mare is called *Street Style* and it is currently grazing in a paddock, Barclay hopeful its first race is not that far away.

He continues to help son Dean in his coaching projects. In particular the current academy Dean has set up out at the Kilsyth Tennis Club in Melbourne's eastern suburbs.

Ian's family was always the glue that kept the dream alive. His children were the apples of his eye. In between long hard days on the court, he would love nothing more than coming home to catch up with them. And they had their own international experiences.

On December 2nd 2018, Ian Barclay turned 80 years of age.

Ann Quinn, Pat Cash, Ian and Mark Hartnett   Ian and sister Janet

A fabulous night was held at the Grace Park Tennis Club in Hawthorn early into the New Year to celebrate the milestone. Around 200 friends from several generations gathered to both reminisce and hear some of the many fascinating stories about Barkers and his life. In a fitting celebration of a wonderfully and rich extraordinary life, family members, past playing partners, assistant coaches, current day students, together with 1987 Wimbledon Men's Singles Champion Pat Cash and other friends, all toasted the man treasured by so many. True to form, the well-dressed lithe figure with that familiar white mane of hair could be seen dancing into the wee early hours of the morning, keeping up with those half his age.

Philosophy

Ian Barclay's number one philosophy in life was, and still is, that the harder you work, the luckier you become. He made no secret of it.

Toni-Ann said if his players tried their guts out and left nothing on the court, her dad admired that the most, even at times, ahead of other areas of their games. "Dad was very competitive when it came to playing his own matches, so if required, he wouldn't hesitate to question his own pupil's level of effort. He would constantly remind his students, like he still does today, to be strong in making their line calls and decisions and to stand up for themselves and their rights at all times during matches."

The highly lucrative, yet competitive Men's and Women's professional tennis tour has become a carrot for so many up-and-coming young players around the world. Reaching that level and then staying there needs ruthless determination, hard work and plenty of good fortune along the way. Reaching those heights though cannot be guaranteed.

To this end, Barclay believes that all young players should have a solid education behind them, something to fall back on should those aspirations not be met. "These days it is still possible, but the chances of having a successful career in tennis are almost a million to one. So many countries around the world play the sport and so many young players' desperate family situations reflect the pressure to make it to the top. There have been exceptions, but it's rare. The other issue is staying in school as long as possible. Tennis is such a singular sport, so dropping out of school and taking on home schooling as the alternative can have severe social ramifications."

Passion, Patience and Dedication

Passion, patience, dedication and never-ending encouragement to his young players are words Ann Quinn likes to describe about Barclay. "And we always had a lot of fun too! He was able to communicate to players of all levels and make sure they understood the finer technicalities of the game. He would work tirelessly to make sure they got it right, even if that meant being on the court or watching videos at 11 o'clock at night. A rotation of just a few degrees of the wrist for example, was always picked up and that was long before there was any sophisticated equipment like that available today.

"One of his greatest strengths too is his ability to teach the tactical side of the game. He would be at every tournament, every week of the year, watching his charges play and always giving positive feedback as well as being a shoulder to lean on for the losses too. And he would always turn those losses into great lessons going forward. He would spend hours analysing their matches. No stone was left unturned. His energy and passion for the game and dedication to his charges, even now at 80 years of age, is truly to be admired and greatest of all is his caring heart."

Of his old coach Pat Cash said, "In my time, no one ever said a bad word about Barkers. Even on the senior circuit, as I travel around the world these days, people come up and ask me the name of my old coach, who they remember as being 100 years old when he wasn't, and a really nice man with it. He procured so many contacts around the world.

"He created a trust within those people he could call friends, only too willing to help both he and Jackie out if the need arose. He was a one in a million coach.

"For me, Barker's greatest ability was to teach me how to win points. The time he spent watching me and the other kids at tournaments was phenomenal. He put me into 'A' Grade pennant in Melbourne and spoke to me about how nerve-wracking an experience it would be. Sure enough, that's how it felt at the time. I learned how to play defensive shots, attacking shots, when to stay back and when to come into the net, how to set up the point, then how to finish it off. This information, coming from Barkers was his biggest influence on my game. Also his ability to analyse my matches afterwards. I believe this is something seen less and less from our coaches these days. Many teach the kids how to hit the ball but not many teach the kids how to play the game.

"There aren't the coaches I know around willing to put in that extra effort. His passion for the game and love for the kids is a one-off. There aren't those willing to go to the nth degree to get the best out of their pupils. You need a bit of luck to be successful in anything in life and my luck was when my schoolmate Warren Brennan introduced me to Ian Barclay all those years ago.

"There's no doubt, I don't think I would have made it as a player without Barkers by my side and I'll be forever grateful for that. When I'm back in Melbourne I'll drop in to Ian's to say hello and have a chat. In many ways Barkers was much closer to me than my own father. I spent more time with him than his own son and my mate Dean. That's just the way it was. For lots of years he was like my first father, the most important male figure in my life."

Hartnett believed that the opportunity to play alongside Barclay both in domestic competition and tournaments, was the key that helped speed up the development of both his own and the games of many of Barclay's students.

Will Coghlan believed Barclay contributed much to Australian tennis. "His early trips overseas with Pat Cash and others to learn how to play on European clay courts were well noted, and a major forerunner in today's landscape of junior development. His contribution should be acknowledged in the way he has gone about producing top players. His dedication, hard work, putting in the hundreds of extra hours outside those he was paid for, watching his juniors play tournaments, club matches, watching opposition players to help give his own players important pointers. He is only one of a handful of coaches who has been prepared to put in such an extraordinary amount of time into his pupils."

Coghlan believed that deep down, Barclay having developed one of the all-time classic serve and volley players in Pat Cash is a little disappointed that within the modern game of tennis, the traditional game style has all but disappeared from singles. "Pat's matches often brought together contrasts in styles, where all shots in the game were played and with it much enjoyment, whereas today so many play primarily from the back of the court and it can often be quite a boring affair for spectators."

Coghlan acknowledged that Barclay used his great doubles expertise to teach his young juniors to volley well and laments that as the game today has changed so much, that many of our good young players shy away from the doubles game and thus don't volley particularly well. In coaching Cash, Coghlan believed Barclay was able to make him into a great volleyer himself and developed probably the best smash in world tennis when he was at his peak. He achieved what he set out to do and was in a very fortunate situation in that he had Jackie to support him in his desire to make good players into top players.

Rohan Goetzke reflected, "As a junior player at squad training many years ago, Barkers was always on the court, walking around and making sure you were executing everything correctly. There were no put-downs, only encouragement and motivation. That alone made you feel important, want to be coached by him and want to put everything into your practice. It also made you feel like you were genuinely a part of his group."

Of his father, Dean said, "Dad's ideas and methods of teaching the game have always been simple and easy to comprehend. He would take on pupils, build them up and teach them how to play the game. His success can be measured threefold. Firstly, taking Patrick Cash all the way to the 1987 Wimbledon Men's Singles title, secondly by the number of nationally and internationally ranked juniors he has coached around the world, and thirdly by the players he has coached who have gone on to become successful coaches in their own right."

Of his father, Brad said, "We'll bury Dad on the tennis court ... it's been his domain, his office, his life."

Postscript

Ian Barclay's long-held passion for all sports has undoubtedly helped keep the fire burning for his tennis coaching. His long journey in the world of tennis now entitles him to do the other things in life. He still loves tennis, enjoys teaching the game and enjoys making a difference to someone's life. In many ways he can be aligned to a big company executive, never having any desire to stagnate and remain in his comfort zone. He has always needed to be challenged.

I, along with so many others, can count myself extremely fortunate to have walked alongside, been taught and mentored by this great man for all these years. It has been a privilege to recount Barkers' stories from wonderful people all over the world.

Tennis has been truly blessed to have Ian Lawrence Barclay grace its courts.

Mike Spruzen

Epilogue

"As I reflect back on the last 50 years on the tennis court, the little things, I believe, that have contributed to my success as a coach in many ways have revolved around the people I have been associated with.

To have the Heatherdale Tennis Club support me as it did in my early grassroots coaching career was instrumental in me moving forward with my pet love, that being junior tennis development.

To have had pupils and assistant coaches across two countries demonstrate the level of work ethic, loyalty, dedication, willingness and desire to learn, commitment and respect for both themselves and me, it speaks volumes for them as people.

Tennis coaching embraces many tangible and intangible qualities: teaching the game, watching pupils compete, analysing, correcting, improving, seeking perfection, evolving, caring, connecting, relating, having passion and encouraging but to name a handful.

If we in the industry are to look at ourselves in the mirror and measure ourselves against some of these, only then can we judge if we are really fulfilling our duty to the game."

Ian Barclay

Index

Agassi, Andre, 105
Anger, Matt, 59
Antonitsch, Alex, 105
Archutowski, Victor, 108
Arendt, Nicole, 160
Atkins, Max, 170
Auckland, James, 112
Austin, Laura, 163
Australian Open, 24
Avvenire Cup, 45
Baily, James, 111
Barabanschikova, Olga, 129
Barclay, Arthur, 10
Barclay, Ethel, 10
Barclay, Ian, 6
Barclay, Ivy, 10
Barclay, Janet, 10
Barclay, Jessica, 10
Barclay, Leo, 12
Barclay, Roy, 10
Barclay, Toni-Ann, 24
Barty, Ashleigh, 158
Beare, Peter, 33
Becker, Boris, 86
Beischer, Bill, 138
Bendit, Emily, 107
Benhabiles Tarik, 51
Bisham Abbey, 110
Black, Cara, 120
Bland, Graham, 26
Bland, Peter, 62
Bollittierri, Nick, 108
Bond, Jeff, 81
Booth, Maree, 60
Borg, Bjorn, 46
Borwick, Neil, 104
Bowrey, Bill, 160
Brennan, Barry, 17
Brennan, Warren, 31
Brown, Nick, 102
Bryan, Bob and Mike, 152
Burbridge, Jessie, 164
Butterfield, Bob, 116
Cahill, Darren, 88
Cahill, Norman, 147
Carroll, Daniel, 33
Cash, Bryan, 35
Cash, Patrick, 33
Castle, Andrew, 102
Cawley, Evonne, 91
Champion, Thierry, 107
Chang, Michael, 105

Charlton, Bobby, 120
Childs, Lee, 112
Coghlan, Will, 21
Colinari, Belinda, 145
Connors, Jimmy, 70
Court, Margaret, 75
Courteau, Loic, 51
Cowan, Barry, 111
Crossman, Andrew, 41
Davidson, Trevor, 26
Davydenko, Nikolay, 137
de Castella, Robert, 92
Delgado, Jamie, 112
Denny, Ewen, 26
Dickson, Simon, 112
Doohan, Peter, 87
Drewett, Brad, 87
Dundas, Lou, 32
Dyke, Broderick, 105
Edberg, Stefan, 46
Edgley, Michael, 45
Edmondson, Mark, 60
Edmund, Kyle, 166
Ellis, Howard, 18
Eltingh, Jacco, 168
Emerson, Roy, 24
Enqvist, Thomas, 137
Evert, Chris, 53
Ewart, Ernie, 171
Fitzgerald, John, 60
Ford, David, 132
Forget, Guy, 46
Foster, Andrew, 111
Fowler, Philip, 111
Fraser, John, 16
Fraser, Neale, 16
Frawley, Rod, 53
Freeman, Marciel, 86
Frystenberg, Marius, 152
Fuhrmann, Klaus, 74
Gandolfo, Mike, 61
Gilbert, Brad, 94
Gleeson, Chris, 59
Glynn, John, 5
Goetzke, Rohan, 33
Gonzales, Pancho, 76
Graf, Steffi, 91
Groth, Sam, 166
Guy, Steven, 104
Hafey, Tom, 13
Hargreaves, Mark, 33
Harris, Graham, 53

Hartnett, Mark, 31
Harty, Jamie, 53
Hawke, Bob, 69
Hayes, Jack, 170
Heatherdale Tennis Club, 26
Henman, Tim, 102
Hernandez, Alejandro, 121
Hewitt, Lleyton, 158
Hoad, Lew, 26, 44
Hodgkin, Sharon, 36
Hopman, Harry, 27
Horskins, Wes, 33
Hravek, Hak, 103
Hulbert, Anne, 60
Hunt, Geoff, 31
Hutchins, Paul, 120
Iron Maiden, 93
Jacques, Warren, 102
Jagger, Mick, 93
Jarryd, Anders, 68
Jelen, Eric, 103
Jones, Gavin, 33
Jones, Greg, 166
Kachel, Chris, 149
Kachel, Kim, 149
Kearney, Bert, 24
Kearney, Katrina, 173
Keller, John, 21
Keller, Lisa, 33
Kiernan, Daniel, 112
Kilderry Rob, 160
King, Billie Jean, 72
King, Mike, 17
Kneale, Charles, 40
Kooyong, 24
Kozma, Martin, 57
Krajicek, Richard, 168
Kratzman, Mark, 105
Kuhnen, Patrick, 115
Lane, Tom, 138
Laver, Rod, 30
Leach, Rick, 105
Leconte, Henri, 80
Lee, Martin, 112
Leipus, Natalia, 53
Lendl, Ivan, 46
Lewis, Carl, 82
Lewis, Richard, 111
Lloyd, John, 67
Loccisano, Rocky, 37
Lorzano, Jorge, 97
Macci, Rick, 123
MacDonald, Jan, 47
Mahon, Billy, 18
Mandlikova, Hana, 46
Marciel, Francisco, 97

Massey, Bernie, 16
Masur, Wally, 45
Matkowski, Marin, 152
Mauresmo, Amelie, 129
Mayotte, Tim, 86
McClagan, Miles, 111
McColl, Natalie, 33
McEnroe, John, 70
McKenzie, Ron, 32
McMahon, Noel, 12
McNamara, Peter, 74
McNamee, Paul, 61
McQuillan, Rachel, 108
Meagher, Joanna, 33
Mecir, Miloslav, 46
Melbourne Park, 53
Mellis, Zoe, 163
Melville, Kerry, 48
Miller, Craig, 60
Minter, Elizabeth, 33
Molloy, Gardner, 76
Morgan, Vicki, 171
Morozova, Olga, 114
Morris, Nish, 144
Naidu, Dr Shastra, 144
Naismith, Jacqualene Mary, 23
Naismith, Jimmy, 23
Naismith, Kay, 23
Nelson, James, 112
Neville-Smith, Richard, 140
Newcombe, John, 21
Noah, Yannick, 60
Norman, Greg, 91
Novacek, Karel, 54
Nystrom, Joakim, 68
O'Connor, Ray, 17
O'Donnell, Simon, 80
O'Reilly, Barry, 173
Occleshaw, Ian, 147
Osborne, Geoff, 23
Ostapenko, Jelena, 164
Osterrieth, Alex, 111
Pernfors, Mikael, 83
Perott, Lindsay, 16
Pioline, Cedric, 108
Puerto, Mariano, 121
Pugh, Jim, 105
Quinn, Ann, 39
Rafter, Pat, 91
Ragg, Philip, 33
Randall, Bernadette, 36
Reva, Natasha, 67
Riby, Ben, 112
Riggs, Bobby, 75
Roche, Tony, 30
Rogers, Keith, 47

Rosewall, Ken, 30
Ruffels, Ray, 21
Rusedski, Greg, 137
Ryan, Tony, 27
Sabbin, Lee, 111
Sampras, Pete, 99
Sanchez, Emilio, 54
Sangster, Mike, 21
Savchenko, Larisa, 67
Schapers, Michiel, 87
Schofield, Mark, 111
Segura, Pancho, 71
Sherwood, David, 112
Shoet, Gerald, 18
Siemerink, Jan, 168
Simmonson, Hans, 68
Sivaratnam, Shyan, 164
Slattery, Brian, 16
Smith, Margaret, 48
Smith, Peter, 70
Spruzen, Geoff, 29
Spruzen, Mike, 81
Steeb, Carl Uwe, 115
Stich, Michael, 169
Stickler, Gary, 160
Stone, Allan, 21
Stone, Geoff, 109
Stosur, Sam, 158
Stubbs, Colin, 23
Sundstrom, Henrik, 60
Super 10s, 153
Taylor, Roger, 21
TCAV Coach of the Year award, 147

TCAV Hall of Fame, 147
Tennis Australia, 84
Tennis Coaches Association of Victoria, 44
Tennis Victoria, 109
Thomas, Andrew, 140
Thorpe, Keith, 14
Tregonning, Don, 147
Trotman, James, 111
Turner, James, 102
US Open, 71
van der Westhuizen, Jaco, 125
Vaughan, Aidan, 162
Vear, Paul, 32
Victorian Spirit of Tennis Award, 147
Vidats, Reka, 129
Warwick, Kim, 60
Washington, MaliVai, 169
Wearne, Brian, 38
Webster, Mike, 172
Werdel, Marianne, 67
White, Charlie, 25
Whitehouse, Wesley, 125
Wilander, Mats, 46
Williams, Richard, 123
Wimbledon, 35
Windahl, Jorgen, 60
Wood, Steve, 138
Woodbridge, Todd, 104
Woodforde, Mark, 43
Yates, Miranda, 53
Youl, Simon, 97
Zivojinovic, Slobodan, 103
Zuker, David, 81

www.ingramcontent.com/pod-product-compliance
Lightning Source LLC
Chambersburg PA
CBHW081110080526
44587CB00021B/3523